Outlook 2010: Basic

Instructor's Edition

Outlook 2010: Basic

President, Axzo Press:	Jon Winder
Vice President, Product Development:	Charles G. Blum
Vice President, Operations:	Josh Pincus
Director of Publishing Systems Development:	Dan Quackenbush
Developmental Editors:	Tim Poulsen, Andrew LaPage
Copyeditor:	Catherine Oliver
Keytester:	Cliff Coryea

Trademarks

ILT Series is a trademark of Axzo Press.

Some of the product names and company names used in this book have been used for identification purposes only and may be trademarks or registered trademarks of their respective manufacturers and sellers.

Disclaimer

We reserve the right to revise this publication and make changes from time to time in its content without notice.

ISBN 10: 1-4260-2115-1
ISBN 13: 978-1-4260-2115-2

Printed in the United States of America

1 2 3 4 5 6 7 8 9 10 GL 13 12 11

What is the Microsoft ® Office Specialist Program?

The Microsoft Office Specialist Program enables candidates to show that they have something exceptional to offer – proven expertise in certain Microsoft programs. Recognized by businesses and schools around the world, over 4 million certifications have been obtained in over 100 different countries. The Microsoft Office Specialist Program is the only Microsoft-approved certification program of its kind.

What is the Microsoft Office Specialist Certification?

The Microsoft Office Specialist certification validates through the use of exams that you have obtained specific skill sets within the applicable Microsoft Office programs and other Microsoft programs included in the Microsoft Office Specialist Program. The candidate can choose which exam(s) they want to take according to which skills they want to validate.

The available Microsoft Office Specialist Program exams include*:
- Using Windows Vista®
- Using Microsoft® Office Word 2007
- Using Microsoft® Office Word 2007 - Expert
- Using Microsoft® Office Excel® 2007
- Using Microsoft® Office Excel® 2007 - Expert
- Using Microsoft® Office PowerPoint® 2007
- Using Microsoft® Office Access® 2007
- Using Microsoft® Office Outlook® 2007
- Using Microsoft SharePoint® 2007

The Microsoft Office Specialist Program 2010 exams will include*:
- Microsoft Word 2010
- Microsoft Word 2010 Expert
- Microsoft Excel® 2010
- Microsoft Excel® 2010 Expert
- Microsoft PowerPoint® 2010
- Microsoft Access® 2010
- Microsoft Outlook® 2010
- Microsoft SharePoint® 2010

What does the Microsoft Office Specialist Approved Courseware logo represent?

The logo indicates that this courseware has been approved by Microsoft to cover the course objectives that will be included in the relevant exam. It also means that after utilizing this courseware, you may be better prepared to pass the exams required to become a certified Microsoft Office Specialist.

For more information:

To learn more about Microsoft Office Specialist exams, visit www.microsoft.com/learning/msbc

To learn about other Microsoft approved courseware from Axzo Press, visit http://www.axzopress.com.

* The availability of Microsoft Office Specialist certification exams varies by Microsoft program, program version and language. Visit www.microsoft.com/learning for exam availability.

Microsoft, Access, Excel, the Office Logo, Outlook, PowerPoint, SharePoint, and Windows Vista are either registered trademarks or trademarks of Microsoft Corporation in the United States and/or other countries. The Microsoft Office Specialist logo and the Microsoft Office Specialist Approved Courseware logo are used under license from Microsoft Corporation.

Contents

Introduction   **iii**

Topic A: About the manual... iv

Topic B: Setting student expectations ix

Topic C: Classroom setup.. xiii

Topic D: Support.. xxii

Getting started   **1-1**

Topic A: The program window... 1-2

Topic B: Outlook Today 1-20

Topic C: Getting help 1-25

Unit summary: Getting started 1-27

E-mail   **2-1**

Topic A: Reading messages 2-2

Topic B: Creating and sending messages 2-6

Topic C: Working with messages 2-20

Topic D: Handling attachments 2-30

Unit summary: E-mail... 2-38

E-mail management   **3-1**

Topic A: Setting message options... 3-2

Topic B: Managing junk e-mail 3-15

Topic C: Using Search folders 3-19

Topic D: Printing messages and attachments 3-22

Unit summary: E-mail management.. 3-25

Contacts   **4-1**

Topic A: Working with contacts.. 4-2

Topic B: Using contact groups 4-17

Topic C: Using the People Pane 4-23

Unit summary: Contacts... 4-30

Tasks   **5-1**

Topic A: Working with tasks... 5-2

Topic B: Managing tasks 5-12

Unit summary: Tasks 5-22

Appointments and events   **6-1**

Topic A: Creating and sending appointments.............................. 6-2

Topic B: Modifying appointments... 6-12

Topic C: Working with events 6-16

Topic D: Using Calendar views 6-20

Unit summary: Appointments and events 6-32

Meeting requests and responses   **7-1**

Topic A: Scheduling meetings... 7-2

Topic B: Managing meetings.. 7-20

Unit summary: Meeting requests and responses...7-26

Course summary   **S-1**
Topic A: Course summary.. S-2
Topic B: Continued learning after class.. S-3

Glossary   **G-1**

Index   **I-1**

Introduction

After reading this introduction, you will know how to:

A Use ILT Series manuals in general.

B Use prerequisites, a target student description, course objectives, and a skills inventory to properly set students' expectations for the course.

C Set up a classroom to teach this course.

D Get support for setting up and teaching this course.

Topic A: About the manual

ILT Series philosophy

Our goal is to make you, the instructor, as successful as possible. To that end, our manuals facilitate students' learning by providing structured interaction with the software itself. While we provide text to help you explain difficult concepts, the hands-on activities are the focus of our courses. Leading the students through these activities will teach the skills and concepts effectively.

We believe strongly in the instructor-led class. For many students, having a thinking, feeling instructor in front of them will always be the most comfortable way to learn. Because the students' focus should be on you, our manuals are designed and written to facilitate your interaction with the students, and not to call attention to manuals themselves.

We believe in the basic approach of setting expectations, then teaching, and providing summary and review afterwards. For this reason, lessons begin with objectives and end with summaries. We also provide overall course objectives and a course summary to provide both an introduction to and closure on the entire course.

Our goal is your success. We encourage your feedback in helping us to continually improve our manuals to meet your needs.

Manual components

The manuals contain these major components:

- Table of contents
- Introduction
- Units
- Course summary
- Glossary
- Index

Each element is described below.

Table of contents

The table of contents acts as a learning roadmap for you and the students.

Introduction

The introduction contains information about our training philosophy and our manual components, features, and conventions. It contains target student, prerequisite, objective, and setup information for the specific course. Finally, the introduction contains support information.

Units

Units are the largest structural component of the actual course content. A unit begins with a title page that lists objectives for each major subdivision, or topic, within the unit. Within each topic, conceptual and explanatory information alternates with hands-on activities. Units conclude with a summary comprising one paragraph for each topic, and an independent practice activity that gives students an opportunity to practice the skills they've learned.

The conceptual information takes the form of text paragraphs, exhibits, lists, and tables. The activities are structured in two columns, one telling students what to do, the other providing explanations, descriptions, and graphics. Throughout a unit, instructor notes are found in the left margin.

Course summary

This section provides a text summary of the entire course. It is useful for providing closure at the end of the course. The course summary also indicates the next course in this series, if there is one, and lists additional resources students might find useful as they continue to learn about the software.

Glossary

The glossary provides definitions for all of the key terms used in this course.

Index

The index at the end of this manual makes it easy for you and your students to find information about a particular software component, feature, or concept.

Manual conventions

We've tried to keep the number of elements and the types of formatting to a minimum in the manuals. We think this aids in clarity and makes the manuals more classically elegant looking. But there are some conventions and icons you should know about.

Instructor note/icon

Item	Description
Italic text	In conceptual text, indicates a new term or feature.
Bold text	In unit summaries, indicates a key term or concept. In an independent practice activity, indicates an explicit item that you select, choose, or type.
`Code font`	Indicates code or syntax.
`Longer strings of ▶ code will look ▶ like this.`	In the hands-on activities, any code that's too long to fit on a single line is divided into segments by one or more continuation characters (▶). This code should be entered as a continuous string of text.
	In the left margin, provide tips, hints, and warnings for the instructor.
Select **bold item**	In the left column of hands-on activities, bold sans-serif text indicates an explicit item that you select, choose, or type.
Keycaps like ↵ ENTER	Indicate a key on the keyboard you must press.
	Warnings prepare instructors for potential classroom management problems.
	Tips give extra information the instructor can share with students.
	Setup notes provide a realistic business context for instructors to share with students, or indicate additional setup steps required for the current activity.
	Projector notes indicate that there is a PowerPoint slide for the adjacent content.

Instructor notes.

⚠ *Warning icon.*

TIPS ✓ *Tip icon.*

▱ *Setup icon.*

◪ *Projector icon.*

Hands-on activities

The hands-on activities are the most important parts of our manuals. They are divided into two primary columns. The "Here's how" column gives short directions to the students. The "Here's why" column provides explanations, graphics, and clarifications. To the left, instructor notes provide tips, warnings, setups, and other information for the instructor only. Here's a sample:

Do it!

A-1: Creating a commission formula

Here's how	Here's why
1 Open Sales	This is an oversimplified sales compensation worksheet. It shows sales totals, commissions, and incentives for five sales reps.
2 Observe the contents of cell F4		F4	▼		=	=E4*C_Rate	 The commission rate formulas use the name "C_Rate" instead of a value for the commission rate.

Take the time to make sure your students understand this worksheet. We'll be here a while.

For these activities, we have provided a collection of data files designed to help students learn each skill in a real-world business context. As students work through the activities, they will modify and update these files. Of course, students might make a mistake and therefore want to re-key the activity starting from scratch. To make it easy to start over, students will rename each data file at the end of the first activity in which the file is modified. Our convention for renaming files is to add the word "My" to the beginning of the file name. In the above activity, for example, students are using a file called "Sales" for the first time. At the end of this activity, they would save the file as "My sales," thus leaving the "Sales" file unchanged. If students make mistakes, they can start over using the original "Sales" file.

In some activities, however, it might not be practical to rename the data file. Such exceptions are indicated with an instructor note. If students want to retry one of these activities, you will need to provide a fresh copy of the original data file.

PowerPoint presentations

Each unit in this course has an accompanying PowerPoint presentation. These slide shows are designed to support your classroom instruction while providing students with a visual focus. Each presentation begins with a list of unit objectives and ends with a unit summary slide. We strongly recommend that you run these presentations from the instructor's station as you teach this course. A copy of PowerPoint Viewer is included, so it is not necessary to have PowerPoint installed on your computer.

The ILT Series PowerPoint add-in

The CD also contains a PowerPoint add-in that enables you to do two things:

- Create slide notes for the class
- Display a control panel for the Flash movies embedded in the presentations

To load the PowerPoint add-in:

1   Copy the Course_ILT.ppa file to a convenient location on your hard drive.
2   Start PowerPoint.
3   Choose Tools, Macro, Security to open the Security dialog box. On the Security Level tab, select Medium (if necessary), and then click OK.
4   Choose Tools, Add-Ins to open the Add-Ins dialog box. Then, click Add New.
5   Browse to and double-click the Course_ILT.ppa file, and then click OK. A message box will appear, warning you that macros can contain viruses.
6   Click Enable Macros. The Course_ILT add-in should now appear in the Available Add-Ins list (in the Add-Ins dialog box). The "x" in front of Course_ILT indicates that the add-in is loaded.
7   Click Close to close the Add-Ins dialog box.

After you complete this procedure, a new toolbar will be available at the top of the PowerPoint window. This toolbar contains a single button labeled "Create SlideNotes." Click this button to generate slide-notes files in both text (.txt) and Excel (.xls) format. By default, these files will be saved to the folder that contains the presentation. If the PowerPoint file is on a CD-ROM or in some other location to which the slide-notes files cannot be saved, you will be prompted to save the presentation to your hard drive and try again.

When you run a presentation and come to a slide that contains a Flash movie, you will see a small control panel in the lower-left corner of the screen. You can use this panel to start, stop, and rewind the movie, or to play it again.

Topic B: Setting student expectations

Properly setting students' expectations is essential to your success. This topic will help you do that by providing:

- Prerequisites for this course
- A description of the target student
- A list of the objectives for the course
- A skills assessment for the course

Course prerequisites

Students taking this course should be familiar with personal computers and the use of a keyboard and a mouse. Furthermore, this course assumes that students have completed the following course or have equivalent experience:

- *Windows 7: Basic, Windows Vista: Basic*, or *Windows XP: Basic*

Target student

The target student for the course is an individual who wants to learn the basic features of Outlook 2010 and use them to create and manage e-mail messages, contacts, appointments, meetings, and tasks.

Course objectives

You should share these overall course objectives with your students at the beginning of the day. This will give the students an idea about what to expect, and it will help you identify students who might be misplaced. Students are considered misplaced when they lack the prerequisite knowledge or when they already know most of the subject matter to be covered.

Note: In addition to the general objectives listed below, specific Microsoft Office Specialist exam objectives are listed at the beginning of each topic (where applicable) and are highlighted by instructor notes.

After completing this course, students will know how to:

- Identify elements of the Outlook environment; use and customize Outlook Today; and use the Outlook Help system.
- Read, create, and send e-mail messages; reply to, format, and check spelling in messages; forward, delete, and restore messages; and work with attachments.
- Set delivery options for messages; flag messages; request a read receipt; specify settings for controlling junk e-mail; set up Search folders; and print messages.
- Use the Contacts folder to add, modify, and organize business and personal contacts; customize an electronic business card; create contact groups (distribution lists); and use the People Pane to view contact details.
- Use the Tasks folder to add, edit, and mark tasks; assign tasks; accept or decline a task request; send an update; and track an assigned task.
- Use the Calendar to create single and recurring appointments; change and delete appointments; add events and holidays to the Calendar; and change views.
- Use the Calendar to schedule meetings; read and respond to meeting requests; reserve resources; manage meeting responses; and update and cancel meetings.

Skills inventory

Use the following form to gauge students' skill levels entering the class (students have copies in the introductions of their student manuals). For each skill listed, have students rate their familiarity from 1 to 5, with 5 being the most familiar. Emphasize that this is not a test. Rather, it is intended to provide students with an idea of where they're starting from at the beginning of class. If a student is wholly unfamiliar with all the skills, he or she might not be ready for the class. A student who seems to understand all of the skills, on the other hand, might need to move on to the next course in the series.

Skill	1	2	3	4	5
Identifying elements of the Outlook window					
Using the Navigation pane					
Using the Reading pane					
Using the To-Do Bar					
Accessing folders from Outlook Today					
Customizing Outlook Today					
Using the Outlook Help window					
Previewing and reading messages					
Creating, formatting, and sending messages					
Checking a message's spelling					
Replying to and forwarding messages					
Deleting and restoring messages					
Sending and forwarding attachments					
Compressing large image attachments					
Previewing and saving attachments					
Defining delivery options					
Flagging an e-mail message					
Using delivery and read receipts					
Adding senders to the Blocked Senders or Safe Senders lists					
Marking a message as not junk					
Changing options for managing junk e-mail					

Skill	1	2	3	4	5
Setting up and using a Search folder					
Customizing the page setup for printing					
Printing messages and attachments					
Adding and modifying contacts					
Attaching items to a contact					
Adding a contact from the same company as a previous contact					
Sending and saving contacts					
Creating and using a contact group (distribution list)					
Updating a contact group					
Printing contacts					
Customizing an electronic business card					
Creating and deleting tasks					
Editing tasks					
Adding recurring tasks					
Marking a task as completed					
Attaching a task to a message					
Assigning tasks					
Accepting a task request					
Sending task status reports					
Tracking assigned tasks					
Printing tasks					
Setting up appointments					
Adding and modifying recurring appointments					
Deleting and restoring appointments					
Changing the work day times in the Calendar					
Displaying multiple time zones					
Adding events					

Skill	1	2	3	4	5
Adding holidays to the calendar					
Printing calendars					
Creating and sending meeting requests					
Adding and modifying recurring meetings					
Reading and accepting a meeting request					
Responding to a New Time Proposed message					
Declining a meeting request					
Reviewing meeting responses					
Updating a meeting					
Adding meeting attendees					
Canceling meetings					

Topic C: Classroom setup

All our courses assume that each student has a personal computer to use during the class. Our hands-on approach to learning requires that they do. This topic gives information on how to set up the classroom to teach this course.

Hardware requirements

The classroom server should have:

- A keyboard and a mouse
- At least 1.4 GHz 64-bit processor (2 GHz or faster recommended)
- At least 1 GB RAM (2 GB or greater recommended)
- At least 50 GB hard drive
- A DVD-ROM drive
- SVGA monitor at 1024×768

The instructor computer and each student computer should have:

- A keyboard and a mouse
- At least 1 GHz 32-bit or 64-bit processor
- At least 1 GB RAM
- At least 50 GB hard drive with at least 15 GB of available space
- A DVD-ROM drive
- A graphics card that supports DirectX 9 graphics with:
  - WDDM driver
  - 128 MB of graphics memory (minimum)
  - Pixel Shader 2.0 in hardware
  - 32 bits per pixel
- SVGA monitor

Software requirements

You will need the following software:

- Windows Server 2008 Standard 64-bit Edition with Service Pack 2
- Windows 7 Professional
- Microsoft Exchange Server 2010 Standard Edition
- Microsoft Outlook 2010, which is included with the Microsoft Office 2010 Home and Business, Standard, Professional, and Professional Plus editions

Network requirements

The following network components and connectivity are also required for this course:

- Internet access, for the following purposes:
  - Downloading the latest critical updates and service packs from www.windowsupdate.com
  - Completing activities throughout the course
  - Downloading the Student Data files from www.axzopress.com (if necessary)
- A static IPv4 address for the classroom server on the same subnet as the student and instructor computers. You will need a DHCP server available on that subnet and a pool of addresses sufficient for the instructor and student computers.
- A network printer that student can access from the classroom.

Classroom setup instructions

Classroom server installation

Before you teach this course, you will need to perform the following steps to set up the classroom server.

1   Install Windows Server 2008 Standard, using the following information:

    a   Don't go online to get the latest updates for installation.

    b   Select the appropriate language, time and currency format, and keyboard or input method.

    c   Select Windows Server 2008 Standard (Full Installation).

    d   Accept the license agreement.

    e   Choose a custom installation. Create at least a 40 GB partition and format it as NTFS.

    f   When prompted, enter and confirm a password of **!pass1234** for the Administrator account.

    g   If prompted, set the network location to Work.

2   If necessary, change your display settings to 1024×768 or 1280×1024.

3   Configure the server, using the Initial Configuration Tasks window.

    a   Set the correct time zone and time.

    b   Configure networking for the Local Area Connection:

        – If necessary, install a driver for the network adapter.

        – Specify the appropriate static IPv4 addressing parameters, including an IP address, subnet mask, and default gateway address, for your classroom network.

    c   Name the computer **winserver**. Restart when prompted.

    d   Install the Web Server (IIS) role.

        i   Under Customize This Server, click Add roles, and click Next.

        ii   Select Web Server (IIS). If prompted, click Add Required Features. Click Next twice.

        iii   If prompted, click Next to install default role services.

        iv   Click Install.

    e Install the Active Directory Domain Services role.

        i Under Customize This Server, click Add roles, and click Next.

       ii Select Active Directory Domain Services, and click Next twice. Click Install.

     iii Click "Close this wizard and launch the Active Directory Domain Services Installation Wizard (dcpromo.exe)." Click Next twice.

     iv Select "Create a new domain in a new forest" and click Next.

      v In the FQDN text box, type **outlanderspices.com**, and click Next.

     vi In the Forest functional level list, select Windows Server 2008. Click Next.

    vii Verify that DNS server is selected, and click Next. Click Yes.

   viii Click Next to accept the default locations for the database folder, the log files folder, and the SYSVOL folder.

     ix Enter and confirm **!pass1234** as the restore-mode administrator password. Click Next twice.

      x Check "Reboot on completion."

4 Log back on as Administrator. In the Initial Configuration Tasks window, check "Do not show this window at logon" and click Close.

5 Turn off Internet Explorer Enhanced Security Configuration.

    a In Server Manager, select the Server Manager console root.

    b Under Security Information, click "Configure IE ESC."

    c Under Administrators, select Off. Under Users, select Off. Click OK.

    d Leave Server Manager open.

6 If your copy of Windows Server 2008 Standard Edition didn't include Service Pack 2, install it now. You can do this from Microsoft's Windows Update site. (Use caution when allowing Windows Update to install any files newer than SP2, as this course wasn't keytested using newer patches.)

Exchange Server 2010 installation

1 Insert the Exchange Server DVD into your server's drive.

2 In the AutoPlay dialog box, click Run Setup.exe.

3 Click "Step 1: Install .NET Framework 3.5 SP1" and follow these steps to install the .NET framework:

    a Internet Explorer opens and displays a page at the Microsoft downloads site. Click Download.

    b Click Run to download and run the .NET framework installation file.

    c Click Run again to install the .NET framework.

    d Close all open windows except Exchange Server.

4 Click "Step 2: Install Windows PowerShell v2" and follow these steps to install the PowerShell component:

  a Internet Explorer opens and displays a page at the Microsoft support site. Scroll about halfway down the page to locate the Windows Management Framework Core (WinRM 2.0 and Windows PowerShell 2.0) heading.

  b Download the 64-bit Windows server package by clicking "Download the Windows Management Framework Core for Windows Server 2008 x64 Edition package now."

  c Run and install the Windows Management Framework Core package. Restart when prompted.

5 Use Windows PowerShell to install the required server components:

  a Click Start and choose All Programs, Administrative Tools, Windows PowerShell Modules. If prompted for administrator credentials, enter **Administrator** as the user name and **!pass1234** as the password.

  b Type
    `ServerManagerCmd -ip d:\scripts\Exchange-Typical.xml`
    and press Enter. The script will install various required components.

  c When the script displays <010/100>, press Enter.

  d Close the Windows PowerShell Modules window.

  e Click Start. Beside the Shutdown and Lock buttons, click the triangle button and choose Restart. From the Option list, select Application Installation (Planned). Click OK.

6 Log on as Administrator and then close Server Manager.

7 Use the Windows PowerShell to set the NetTcpPortSharing service to start automatically:

  a Click Start and choose Windows PowerShell Modules.

  b At the prompt, type
    `Set-Service NetTcpPortSharing -StartupType Automatic`
    and press Enter.

  c Type **exit** and press Enter.

8 Install the 2007 Office System Converter: Microsoft Filter Pack by following these steps:

  a Open Internet Explorer. In the Address bar, enter
    http://go.microsoft.com/fwlink/?LinkID=123380

  b Scroll to the bottom of the page. Next to FilterPackx64.exe, click Download.

  c Click Run, and then click Run again. Click Next.

  d Check "I accept the terms in the License Agreement" and click Next.

  e Click OK. Close Internet Explorer.

9 Eject and then insert the Exchange DVD. In the AutoPlay dialog box, click Run Setup.exe.

10 Click "Step 3: Choose Exchange Language option." Then click "Install only languages from the DVD."

11 Click "Step 4: Install Microsoft Exchange," click Next, and follow these steps to install Exchange:

a   Select "I accept the terms in the license agreement" and click Next.

b   With No selected in the Error Reporting options, click Next.

c   With Typical Exchange Server Installation selected, click Next.

d   In the "Specify the name for this Exchange organization" box, enter **Outlander Spices**. Click Next.

e   On the Client Settings page, select No (if necessary) and click Next.

f   Click Next (do not check "The Client Access Server role will be Internet-facing").

g   Select "I don't wish to join the program at this time" and click Next.

h   On the Readiness Checks page, you will likely receive a warning message about not installing Exchange 2007 server roles. That is fine. If you receive any failure messages, correct the problems by following the on-screen instructions. You can leave this page of the wizard open and click Retry after correcting problems.

i   Click Install. The Progress page will display the installation progress. Depending on the speed of your server, the installation could take as much as an hour to finish.

j   Clear the checkbox to display the Exchange Management console. Click Finish.

12 Click "Step 5: Get critical updates for Microsoft Exchange" and follow these steps to install the updates:

a   If necessary, click "I agree to the Terms of Use for Microsoft Update."

b   Click Next.

c   Select Use Recommended Settings, and click Install to install Microsoft Update.

d   Click "Get critical updates for Microsoft Exchange" to restart the update process. Check for new updates. If updates are found for Microsoft Exchange, install them, following the on-screen instructions. Restart if prompted.

13 Click Close. Remove the DVD from your drive.

14 Click Start and choose All Programs. If you do not see a Microsoft Exchange Server 2010 menu option, then not all components were installed. Insert the Exchange DVD in your drive and run Setup.exe. When prompted, make sure that "Mailbox server," "Client Access server," and "Hub Transport server" are checked. Check the missing roles and proceed again through the installation wizard to install them.

Creating user accounts for students

You will need to create a user account for yourself and for each student in class. Name your account **Instructor**, and name each student account **Student##** where ## is a unique number you assign to each account.

During class, students will work in pairs to complete some activities. If you have an odd number of students, you can work with one of the students as his or her partner. If you have an even number of students, you will need a partner user account (though not a computer) to key through the partnered activities. If necessary, create a **Student999** account to use as the instructor's partner with a class of an even number of students.

For each account, follow these steps:

1   In Server Manager, expand Roles, Active Directory Domain Services, Active Directory Users and Computers, and the outlanderspices.com domain.

2   In the Users folder, right-click a blank space and choose New, User.

3   Leave the First Name and Initials fields blank. In the Last Name and User logon name boxes, enter the account name (for example, **Instructor** or **Student##**).

4   Click Next.

5   Enter and confirm a password of **!pass1234**. Uncheck "User must change password at next logon." Check "User cannot change password" and "Password never expires."

6   Click Next. Click Finish.

7   After you have created all of the accounts, close Server Manager.

Creating mailboxes for students

Mailbox creation in Exchange Server 2010 is not managed through Active Directory, as was done with previous versions of the software. To create mailboxes, you must use an Exchange-specific tool.

1   On the Exchange server, click Start and choose All Programs, Microsoft Exchange Server 2010, Exchange Management Console.

2   Expand Microsoft Exchange on-Premises (winserver.outlanderspices.com).

3   Select Recipient Configuration.

4   In the middle pane, right-click and choose New Mailbox.

5   With User Mailbox selected, click Next.

6   Select Existing users. Click Add.

7   Select all of the accounts you added (use Ctrl+click or Shift+click to select them all) and click OK. Click Next.

8   Click Next. Click New to create a mailbox for each user you selected.

9   Click Finish.

Creating mailboxes for resources

Students will create meeting requests that schedule resources, such as rooms and equipment. Follow these steps to create mailboxes corresponding to those resources:

1   In the middle pane, under the mailboxes you just created, right-click and choose New Mailbox.

2   Select Room Mailbox and click Next.

3   Click Next.

4   Enter the following user account details and then click Next:

    Name: **Conference Room A**

    User logon name: **conf_room_A**

    Password: **P@ssword**

5   In the Alias box, enter **CR_A** and then click Next.

6   Click Next, click New, and then click Finish to create the mailbox.

7   Close the Exchange Management Console.

Setting up the instructor and student computers

You will need to perform the following steps to set up the instructor computer and each student computer:

1   Install Windows 7 on an NTFS partition according to the software manufacturer's instructions, following these additional detail steps:

    a   If prompted, click the button specifying to go online and get the latest updates.

    b   In the Set Up Windows dialog box, in the "Type a user name" box, type **Admin**.

    c   In the "Type a computer name" box, type **Computer##** to match the user account names you created for the students. Use **Instructor** for your computer's name.

    d   Click Next. Enter and confirm a password of **!pass**. In the Password Hint box, type **Exclamation abbreviation**.

    e   Click Next. Enter your Windows 7 product key and click Next.

    f   On the "Help protect your computer and improve Windows automatically" page, click "Use recommended settings."

    g   From the Time zone list, select your time zone, and verify the accuracy of the current time. Edit the time if necessary.

    h   Click Next. On the Windows networking page, select Work. Windows completes the setup and displays the desktop.

2   Configure each computer to use your classroom server as the DNS server. To do so:

    a   In the notification area of the taskbar, right-click the Network icon and choose Open Network and Sharing Center.

    b   In the "View your active networks" section, beside Connections, click Local Area Connection.

    c   Click Properties.

    d   Select Internet Protocol Version 4 (TCP/IPv4) and click Properties.

    e   Select "Use the following DNS server addresses." In the Preferred DNS server box, enter your classroom server's IP address.

    f   Click OK, click Close twice, and close the Network and Sharing Center.

3   On each computer, join the classroom domain by following these steps:

    a   Click Start. Right-click Computer and choose Properties.

    b   In the "Computer name, domain, and workgroup settings" section, click Change Settings.

    c   Click Change.

    d   Beneath Member of, select Domain and enter **outlanderspices.com**. Click OK.

    e   When prompted for credentials, enter the domain administrator's user name and password. If you followed the setup notes described previously, the credentials should be Administrator and !pass1234.

    f   Click OK. Then restart the computer using the prompts.

4 From the student and instructor computers, log onto the domain:

   a Click Switch User and then click Other User.

   b Enter the user name associated with the computer (for example, enter Student01 on Computer01).

   c Enter **!pass1234** as the password and click the logon arrow.

5 Install Microsoft Office 2010 according to the software manufacturer's instructions, as follows:

   a Enter the domain Administrator user name and password if prompted. When prompted for the CD key, enter the code included with your software.

   b Perform a custom installation.

   c For Microsoft Outlook, Microsoft Word, Office Shared Features, and Office Tools, click the arrow and choose "Run all from My Computer."

   d Set all *except* the following to Not Available: Microsoft Outlook, Microsoft Word, Office Shared Features, and Office Tools.

   e Click Install Now.

   f On the last screen of the Office 2010 installer, click Continue Online. Internet Explorer displays the Office Online Web site, and the installer window closes.

   g On the Office Online Web page, click the Downloads tab. Download and install any available updates.

   h Close any open windows.

6 On each computer, configure Outlook to connect to the corresponding student account mailbox. For example, on Computer01, connect Outlook to the Student01 mailbox.

   a Click Start and choose All Programs, Microsoft Office, Microsoft Outlook 2010.

   b Click Next. Click Next again.

   c Account information should be acquired automatically from the domain. Click Next.

   d If you're prompted with a Security Alert about a problem with the site's security, follow these steps to install the certificate on the student computer:

      i Click View Certificate.

      ii Click Install Certificate. Click Next twice.

      iii Click Finish. Click Yes.

      iv Click OK twice.

      v Click Yes to close the Security Alert dialog box.

   e Click Finish.

   f In the User Name dialog box, enter a name and initials for the student. For example, in the Name box, enter **Student Number ##**, and in the Initials box, enter **SN##**, where ## is the user's account number. Click OK.

   g In the Help Protect and Improve Microsoft Office section, select Use Recommended Settings. Click OK.

   h In the User Account Control dialog box, enter **Administrator** and **!pass1234** and click Yes.

   i Close Microsoft Outlook.

7 Connect each computer to the network printer, installing printer drivers as necessary. Ensure that students have sufficient permissions to print documents and that there is a sufficient paper supply.

8 If you have the data disc that came with this manual, locate the Student Data folder on it and copy it to the desktop of each student computer.

If you don't have the data disc, you can download the Student Data files for the course:

    a Connect to www.axzopress.com.

    b Under Downloads, click Instructor-Led Training.

    c Browse the subject categories to locate your course. Then click the course title to display a list of available downloads. (You can also access these downloads through our Catalog listings.)

    d Click the link(s) for downloading the Student Data files. You can download the files directly to student machines or to a central location on your own network.

    e Create a folder named Student Data on the desktop of each student computer.

    f Double-click the downloaded zip file(s) and drag the contents into the Student Data folder.

9 From the instructor's computer, send two e-mail messages to each student. Make sure to send copies of the messages to the Instructor account as well. For the first message, use the subject "Welcome to Outlook 2010" and enter a message of your choice in the message area. For the second message, use "Your second message" as the subject and enter a message of your choice.

CertBlaster software

CertBlaster pre- and post-assessment software is available for this course. To download and install this free software, students should complete the following steps:

1 Go to www.axzopress.com.

2 Under Downloads, click CertBlaster.

3 Click the link for Outlook 2010.

4 Save the .EXE file to a folder on your hard drive. (**Note:** If you skip this step, the CertBlaster software will not install correctly.)

5 Click Start and choose Run.

6 Click Browse and navigate to the folder that contains the .EXE file.

7 Select the .EXE file and click Open.

8 Click OK and follow the on-screen instructions. When prompted for the password, enter **c_ol2010**.

Topic D: Support

Your success is our primary concern. If you need help setting up this class or teaching a particular unit, topic, or activity, please don't hesitate to get in touch with us.

Contacting us

Please contact us through our Web site, www.axzopress.com. You will need to provide the name of the course, and be as specific as possible about the kind of help you need.

Instructor's tools

Our Web site provides several instructor's tools for each course, including course outlines and answers to frequently asked questions. To download these files, go to www.axzopress.com. Then, under Downloads, click Instructor-Led Training and browse our subject categories.

Unit 1

Getting started

Unit time: 50 minutes

Complete this unit, and you'll know how to:

A Identify the components of the Outlook environment, and use Outlook panes and folders.

B Use Outlook Today to keep track of your schedule and tasks for today, and customize the Outlook Today page.

C Get help by using the Outlook Help window.

Topic A: The program window

This topic covers the following Microsoft Office Specialist exam objectives for Outlook 2010.

#	Objective
6.1	**Create and manipulate tasks**
	6.1.1 Create a task

Explanation

Outlook is a Microsoft application that you can use to send and receive e-mail. *E-mail* is an electronic message sent from one computer to another. You can also use Outlook as a personal organizer; for example, you can schedule meetings and appointments and keep track of tasks and contacts.

Any e-mail message, contact, or task created in Outlook is called an *item*. Items are stored in folders, such as Inbox, Calendar, Contacts, Tasks, and Notes. These folders help you organize information. You can access the items within each folder by using the buttons in the Outlook window.

Starting the application

You can start Outlook by clicking Start and choosing All Programs, Microsoft Office, Microsoft Office Outlook 2010. Once you have opened the application, Outlook will be added to the Start menu. You can then click the Outlook command to open the program (without clicking All Programs first). You can also point to the Outlook command to display a submenu of commands for Outlook-specific tasks, such as New E-mail Message.

Outlook window elements

The Outlook window contains elements that are common to other Windows-based applications—such as a title bar and a status bar—along with elements that are common to the Microsoft Office 2010 suite of applications. The Office-specific elements, shown in Exhibit 1-1, are the Quick Access toolbar and the Ribbon.

TIPS
The size and arrangement of the buttons on the Ribbon change depending on the width of the application window.

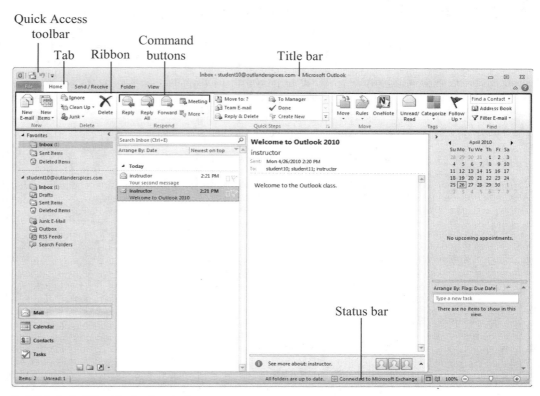

Exhibit 1-1: The Outlook window

The following table describes some of the elements shown in Exhibit 1-1.

Element	Description
Quick Access toolbar	Contains a customizable selection of commonly used buttons. By default, it contains the Send/Receive, Undo, and Customize Quick Access Toolbar buttons.
Ribbon	Contains tabs, each of which contains groups of related commands.
Title bar	Displays the name of the folder being displayed (in Exhibit 1-1, the Inbox of the Student10 user account) and the program name.
Status bar	Displays status information and contains buttons for commands that control the program's display (such as zooming in or out).

The Outlook window also contains elements that are specific to the Outlook application. These elements include a Navigation pane, a Folder pane, a Reading pane, and a To-Do Bar, as shown in Exhibit 1-2. The Navigation pane shows the active pane and a set of buttons for switching the active pane. The Folder pane displays the Folder Contents list. The Reading pane displays e-mail messages. The To-Do Bar displays the Date Navigator, upcoming appointments, and tasks.

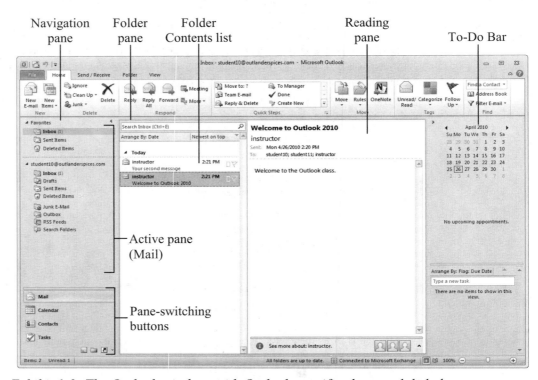

Exhibit 1-2: The Outlook window, with Outlook-specific elements labeled

The following table describes the common elements of the Outlook program window, shown in Exhibit 1-2.

Element	Description
Navigation pane	Provides centralized navigation to all parts of Outlook. Displays the active pane, plus pane-switching buttons.
Pane-switching buttons	Display commonly used panes (such as Mail, Calendar, and Notes) with one click.
Folder pane	Displays the name of the active folder.
Folder Contents list	Displays the contents of the active folder.
Reading pane	Displays the contents of the selected e-mail message. Replaces the Preview Pane used in previous versions of Outlook.
To-Do Bar	Displays the Date Navigator, upcoming appointments, and tasks.

Expanding and minimizing a pane

You can collapse and expand the Navigation pane and To-Do Bar by clicking the sideways-pointing caret-shaped buttons at the top of those panes. If the pane is expanded, clicking the button minimizes the pane. A minimized pane shows summary information and key buttons. If the pane is minimized, clicking the button expands the pane to show its full complement of information and commands.

Resizing a pane

You can increase or decrease the width of an individual pane in the program window. To do so, point to the border of the pane so that the pointer appears as a double-headed arrow, and then drag the border to the left or right.

Do it!

A-1: Exploring the Outlook window

Here's how	Here's why
It might take some time for the Outlook window to appear.	
1 Click **Start** and choose **All Programs**, **Microsoft Office**, **Microsoft Outlook 2010**	To start Microsoft Outlook.
2 Observe the window	As shown in Exhibit 1-1 and Exhibit 1-2. The Outlook window contains various elements, such as the title bar, the Ribbon, the Folder pane, the Navigation pane, the Reading pane, and the To-Do Bar.
3 Observe the Ribbon	
	The Home tab is active. It contains commonly used commands for sending mail, organizing your messages, and managing your calendar.
Click the **Send/Receive** tab	To activate the tab and display commands related to sending and receiving messages.
Click the **Home** tab	To activate the tab.
4 Observe the Navigation pane	
	By default, this pane shows your mail folders. At the top is a customizable list of folders. Below that list are folders associated with your e-mail accounts. Below those folders are buttons, such as Calendar, Contacts, and Tasks, that you can click to display other panes and folders.

5 Observe the Folder pane

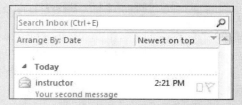

It displays messages stored in the folder that is selected in the Navigation pane (Inbox, in this example). The Folder pane also contains a search box you can use to find items in the folder.

6 Observe the Reading pane

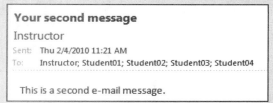

It displays the contents of the message selected in the Folder pane.

7 Observe the To-Do Bar

It displays appointments and tasks that you need to do today.

8 Point to the right border of the Reading pane

The pointer changes to a double-headed arrow.

Drag the border to the right

Press and hold the mouse button, and then move the mouse to decrease the width of the To-Do Bar.

At the top of the To-Do Bar, click ▶

To collapse the To-Do Bar and make more space for the Reading pane.

The Navigation pane

Explanation

The Navigation pane provides centralized navigation to all parts of Outlook. The Navigation pane has two sections, as shown in Exhibit 1-3. The top section displays the active Outlook pane, and the bottom section contains the pane-switching buttons.

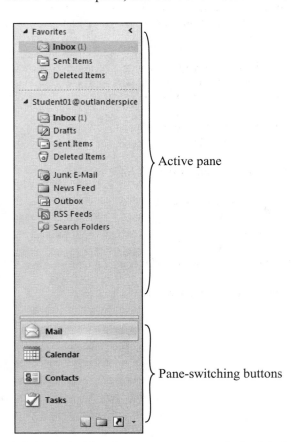

Exhibit 1-3: The Navigation pane with the Mail pane active

Default panes

Outlook provides several default panes where you can access folders or shortcuts specific to each pane. You can access each pane by clicking the pane-switching buttons in the Navigation pane, shown in Exhibit 1-3. The following panes are available by default: Mail, Calendar, Contacts, Tasks, Notes, Folder List, and Shortcuts.

Buttons for the Notes, Folder List, and Shortcuts panes are smaller and are arranged at the very bottom of the Navigation pane, along with the Configure Buttons icon. These buttons are not labeled, but you can point to them to display their names as ScreenTips.

The following table describes the built-in panes that are housed in the Navigation pane.

Pane	Description
Mail	Displays folders designated as Favorites, including your Inbox, Sent Items, and Deleted Items folders, as shown in Exhibit 1-3. Below that section, the pane displays all of your mail folders, including Drafts, Junk E-mail, and Search Folders.
Calendar	Displays the Date Navigator, which is a small calendar that displays the current month. Also displays links to your My Calendars folder, which includes your calendar and possibly other users' calendars.
Contacts	Displays the Contacts and Suggested Contacts folders, plus any extra contacts folders that you create.
Tasks	Displays links to your To-Do List and Tasks folders.
Notes	Displays links to your Notes folders.
Folder List	Displays all of your folders, including Public Folders.
Shortcuts	Contains links to Outlook Today and Microsoft Office Online.
Journal	Displays links to your Journal folders.

Collapsing and expanding the Navigation pane

You can free up space in your Outlook window by collapsing the Navigation pane. To collapse or expand the Navigation pane, either click the sideways-caret symbol (< or >) at the top corner of the pane, or click the View tab and choose Normal, Minimized, or Off from the Navigation Pane menu. The collapsed Navigation pane, as shown in Exhibit 1-4, still provides access to the folders and files that you use most often.

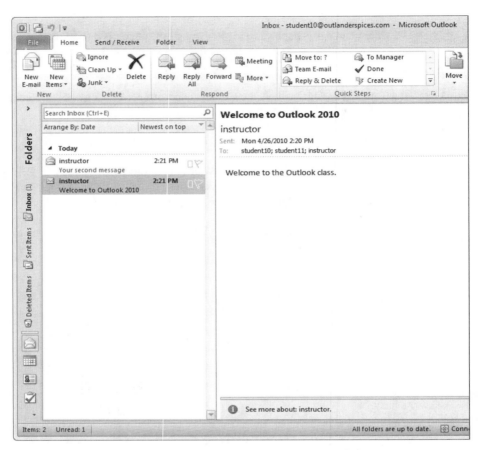

Exhibit 1-4: The Navigation pane, on the left, is collapsed

Do it!   **A-2:   Examining the Navigation pane**

Here's how	Here's why
1 In the Navigation pane, click **Mail**	(If necessary.) To activate the Mail pane. Notice that its contents are divided into Favorites and folders related to your e-mail account.
2 In the Navigation pane, click **Tasks**	To display the Tasks pane and the contents of the Tasks folder, which is empty by default.
3 In the top-right corner of the Navigation pane, click ⟨‹⟩	To collapse the Navigation pane.

The Tasks button is still selected in the Navigation pane.

Click as shown	
	To display the Task list in a flyout menu.
Expand the Navigation pane	Click the sideways-caret icon (>) at the top of the pane.
4 Observe the small icons at the bottom of the Navigation pane	There are several pane-switching icons and the Configure Buttons icon.
Point to each of the icons	
	To view the ScreenTips showing the icons' names.

Help students find the Notes icon.

5 Click	(The Notes icon.) A blank area appears to the right in the Outlook window.
6 Click	(The Folder List icon.) To display the default Outlook folders.
7 Click	(The Shortcuts icon.) The shortcuts menu is empty by default, but contains buttons for adding groups and shortcuts.
8 Click	(The Configure Buttons icon.) A menu is displayed. You can choose commands to show additional panes or configure existing panes.
Click an empty area of the Navigation pane	(For example, click the empty space to the left of the Notes icon.) To close the context menu.

Outlook folders

Explanation   Outlook provides folders in which you can save and store the items you create. You can access these folders by using the default panes within the Navigation pane. You can also access a folder by clicking the Folder List icon in the Navigation pane and then clicking the folder you want. You can use the default folders or create your own folders.

By default, only the most relevant folders for any given pane are displayed. For example, when the Mail pane is active, your Inbox, Drafts, Sent Items, and other folders are visible, but the Calendar and Suggested Contacts folders are not. You can see the full list of folders by clicking the Folder List icon at the bottom of the Navigation pane. Two folder list views are shown in Exhibit 1-5.

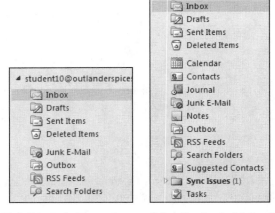

Exhibit 1-5: Two views of the Outlook folder list

The following table describes the default folders.

Outlook lists the key mail-related folders first, followed by the rest in alphabetical order. This table is arranged to match that order.

Folder	Description
\<account address\>	Click your e-mail address to display the Outlook Today page, which provides a snapshot view of your activities planned for the day.
Inbox	You can create, send, receive, delete, and move messages from the Inbox.
Drafts	Stores unfinished items.
Sent Items	Stores copies of items you have sent to other people.
Deleted Items	Stores items that have been deleted from folders.
Calendar	Used to plan and schedule work-related and personal activities, such as appointments, meetings, and events.
Contacts	Stores information about people with whom you frequently communicate.
Journal	Can be used to keep a record of any interaction you want to remember. Stores actions that you choose relating to your contacts and places the actions in a timeline view.
Junk E-mail	Stores messages that were caught by the Junk E-mail filter.
Notes	Provides a place where you can keep reminders about important activities to complete and meetings to attend.
Outbox	Stores items created offline that you want to send the next time you are online.
RSS Feeds	Stores RSS (Really Simple Syndication) subscriptions so you can view data feeds from various news sources and Web logs (blogs).
Search Folders	Displays the results of previously defined search queries.
Suggested Contacts	Stores the e-mail addresses of people with whom you have exchanged e-mail messages but who are not in your Contacts list.
Sync Issues	Stores a list of errors that occur when you are synchronizing Exchange mailbox files with local mailbox files.
Tasks	Used to list and manage the various activities you need to perform.

Do it!

A-3: Accessing folders

Here's how	Here's why
1 Click **Mail**	To activate the Mail pane and display the Inbox folder.
Compare the folder list for your e-mail account to the left-hand graphic in Exhibit 1-5	The mail-related folders are listed first, followed by a selection of key folders related to communications activities.
2 Click	(At the bottom of the Navigation pane.) The Favorites folder is hidden and your account's folder list is expanded to show the full list of folders.
3 In the folder list, click **Drafts**	To view the contents of your Drafts folder. It should be empty. This folder stores e-mail messages you've started but not yet sent.
4 Click **Junk E-Mail**	To view the contents of your Junk E-Mail folder, which would contain messages that Outlook has determined are probably unsolicited commercial e-mail (called "spam").
5 Click **Mail**	To restore the default view of Favorites and account-related folders. Doing so does not select the Inbox folder.
6 Click **Inbox**	To view your Inbox folder.

Context-sensitive tabs

Explanation

The commands available on the various tabs on the Ribbon depend on the folders and panes you select to view. For example, the Home tab contains mail-related commands, as shown in Exhibit 1-6, when the Mail pane is active. But the Home tab shows calendar- and appointment-related commands, as shown in Exhibit 1-7, when the Calendar pane is active.

Exhibit 1-6: The Mail pane's Home tab

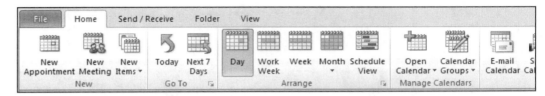

Exhibit 1-7: The Calendar pane's Home tab

Do it!

A-4: Navigating tabs

Here's how	Here's why
1 Observe the Home tab	It contains commands for common e-mail-related actions, such as sending or replying to messages.
2 Click the **Send/Receive** tab	To view its contents. This tab contains commands for processing e-mail.
Click the **Folder** tab	Use commands on this tab to organize your e-mail messages.
3 In the Navigation pane, click **Calendar**	To switch panes. The Calendar pane's Home tab is active. It contains calendar-related commands.
4 Click the **Send/Receive** tab	To view its contents. Now this tab contains commands for processing calendar entries.
Click the **Folder** tab	The Calendar pane's Folder tab is noticeably different from the Mail pane's Folder tab.
5 In the Navigation pane, click **Mail**	To display the Mail pane and its Home tab.

The change of commands is not obvious on this tab.

The Reading pane

Explanation

The Reading pane is displayed only when a mail-related pane or folder is active. When the Mail pane is active, the Reading pane appears between the Folder pane and the To-Do Bar, as shown in Exhibit 1-8. In the Reading pane, you can read the contents of an item, preview and open attachments, follow hyperlinks, use voting buttons, and respond to meeting requests.

If the Reading pane is not displayed, click the View tab, click the Reading Pane button, and choose an option from the menu that appears. Options include Right (default position), Bottom (below the Folder pane), and Off (hidden). If the Reading pane is Off, you can double-click a message to open it in its own window.

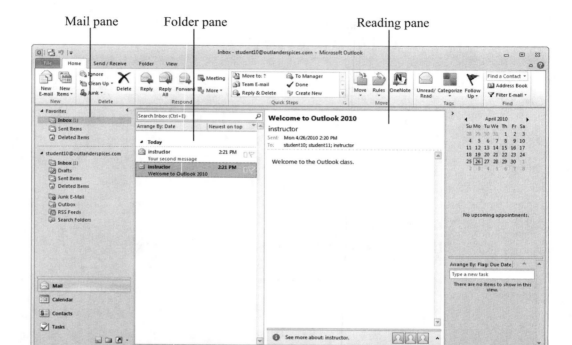

Mail pane   Folder pane   Reading pane

Exhibit 1-8: The location of the Reading pane

Do it!

A-5:   Using the Reading pane

Here's how	Here's why

The date and time of the message will differ from those shown here.

1 Click as shown

✉ instructor	2:21 PM	☐ ▷
Your second message		
✉ instructor	2:21 PM	☐ ▷
Welcome to Outlook 2010		

(The message is in the Folder Contents list.) To select the message with the subject "Welcome to Outlook 2010" from the Instructor.

Observe the Reading pane

A preview of the message content automatically appears in the Reading pane.

2 Click the **View** tab

The icons may appear differently depending on students' screen resolution.

In the Layout group, click **Reading Pane** and choose **Bottom**

Navigation Pane ▾   Reading Pane ▾   To-Do Bar ▾   People Pane ▾

Right
Bottom
Off

2010

The Reading pane appears at the bottom of your window.

3 Click **Reading Pane** and choose **Off**

To close the Reading pane.

Click **Reading Pane** and choose **Right**

To show the Reading pane in its default position.

4 In the Mail pane, click **Sent Items**

To display the contents of the Sent Items folder. The folder is empty, and the Reading pane is blank.

The To-Do Bar

Explanation

Objective 6.1.1

The To-Do Bar provides a way to view your appointments, meetings, and to-do items in a centralized list. A to-do item is any Outlook item—such as a task, e-mail message, or contact—that has been flagged for follow-up. By default, all tasks are flagged for follow-up when they are created. Therefore, whenever you create a task, Outlook automatically creates a to-do item.

The To-Do Bar has three sections, as shown in Exhibit 1-9:

- The top section displays the Date Navigator.
- The second section displays your upcoming appointments and meetings.
- The third section displays your task list and the "Type a new task" box.

Exhibit 1-9: The To-Do Bar

The To-Do Bar is turned on by default. To turn it off, click the View tab, click the To-Do Bar button, and choose Off. To turn the To-Do Bar back on, click To-Do Bar and choose Normal.

If you need a larger Reading pane for reading your messages, you can minimize the To-Do Bar. Either click the caret at the top of the bar, or click the View tab, click To-Do Bar, and choose Minimized. To expand the To-Do Bar, either click the caret at the top of the minimized bar, or click To-Do Bar (on the View tab) and choose Normal.

Do it!

Objective 6.1.1

A-6:   Using the To-Do Bar

Here's how	Here's why
1 Click **Tasks**	To activate the Tasks pane.
2 In the "Type a new task" box, type **Outlook 2010 Class**	Arrange By: Flag: Due Date Outlook 2010 Class (In the To-Do Bar.) You'll create a task for tomorrow.
Press ⏎ ENTER	The task appears in the Task list under Today.
3 Right-click the task	To display a shortcut menu. You'll change the follow-up date for the task.
Choose **Follow Up**, **Tomorrow**	The task now appears in the Task list under Tomorrow.
4 In the Date Navigator, select tomorrow's date	To switch to the Calendar folder. The task appears in the Daily Tasks list at the bottom of the pane.
5 Right-click the task	To display the task shortcut menu.
Choose **Delete**	To delete the task from your Task list.
6 In the Navigation Pane, click **Mail**	The task is no longer displayed in the To-Do Bar.
7 Click the **View** tab	
Click **To-Do Bar** and choose **Off**	To turn off the To-Do Bar.
8 Click **To-Do Bar** and choose **Minimized**	To display the To-Do Bar in its minimized state.
9 Click ◄	To return the To-Do Bar to its normal state.

Topic B: Outlook Today

Explanation

Outlook Today is another way to view a summary of your activities scheduled for the day. The summary displays your events, appointments, meetings, and tasks for the day. To display the Outlook Today view, click your account name (e-mail address) in the Mail or Folder panes.

The Outlook Today page

The Outlook Today page is displayed in the space normally filled by the Folder and Reading panes. It contains three sections—Calendar, Tasks, and Messages—as shown in Exhibit 1-10. Summaries of your activities appear under the respective headings.

By default, under Calendar, you can see scheduled appointments for up to five days. Under Tasks, you'll see a summary of all task items you've created. Under Messages, you'll see the number of unread messages you have (in Inbox), the number of messages you've created but not sent (in Drafts), and the number of sent messages that have not left the computer (in Outbox). You can also click these headings to access the associated folders.

In class, the date and the number of messages in the Inbox might differ from those shown here.

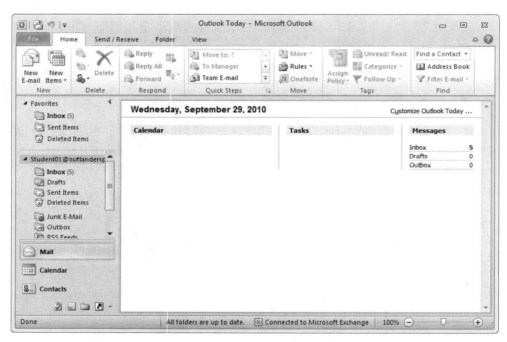

Exhibit 1-10: The Outlook Today page

Do it!   **B-1: Accessing folders from Outlook Today**

Here's how	Here's why
1 Click **Mail**	(If necessary.) In the Navigation pane.
2 Select **Student##@outlanderspices.com**	
	(Where ## is your student number.) To display the Outlook Today page. It provides a summary of the day's plan.
3 Point to **Messages**	Messages
	The pointer's shape changes to a hand, and the text is underlined.
Click **Messages**	To open the Mail pane and the Inbox folder.

Customizing Outlook Today

Explanation

You can customize Outlook Today by using the Customize Outlook Today link, which is in the upper-right corner of the Outlook Today page. The following table describes some of the ways in which you can customize Outlook Today.

Option	Description
Startup	Displays the Outlook Today page when Outlook is opened.
Messages	Displays selected folders in the Messages section.
Calendar	Displays a specified number of days from your calendar in the Calendar section.
Tasks	Displays and sorts the selected tasks in the Tasks section.
Styles	Changes the layout or color scheme of the Outlook Today page.

Make your changes to customize Outlook Today, and then click Save Changes. Your customized settings will take effect immediately.

Do it!

B-2: Customizing Outlook Today

Here's how	Here's why
1 Display Outlook Today	Click your e-mail account name in the Navigation pane.
2 Click as shown	Customize Outlook Today ...
	(On the Outlook Today page.) To open the Customize Outlook Today page in the Outlook window.
3 Check **When starting, go directly to Outlook Today**	(In the Startup section.) To specify that you want Outlook Today to be the startup page.
Under Tasks, select **Today's tasks**	In my task list, show me: ○ All tasks ● Today's tasks ☑ Include tasks with no due date
	To specify that only those tasks you have to perform today should appear in the Tasks list.
From the "Show Outlook Today in this style" list, select **Standard (one column)**	Standard ▾ — Standard / Standard (two column) / Standard (one column) / Summer / Winter
	(You might need to scroll down to find the list.) A preview of the selected layout appears under the list.
4 Click **Save Changes**	(This link appears in the upper-right corner of the Customize Outlook Today page.) To save the changes and close the Customize Outlook Today page. Your changes take effect immediately, and the Calendar, Tasks, and Messages headings appear in a single column.
5 Click the **File** tab and choose **Exit**	(Or click the × in the upper-right corner of the Outlook window.) To close Outlook. Next, you'll restart Outlook to verify that the Outlook Today page opens when you start the program.
6 Start Outlook	(Click Start and choose Microsoft Office Outlook 2010.) The Outlook Today page is now the startup page.

7 Click **Customize Outlook Today**	You will restore the default settings for this page.
Uncheck **When starting, go directly to Outlook Today**	
In the Tasks options, select **All tasks**	To display all tasks in the Tasks list.
From the "Show Outlook Today in this style" list, select **Standard**	To use the default three-column style.
Click **Save Changes**	To restore the default settings for this page.

Topic C: Getting help

Explanation

You can use Outlook's help system to get assistance while you're working. To open the Outlook Help window, shown in Exhibit 1-11, click the Help button, located near the upper-right corner of the Outlook window.

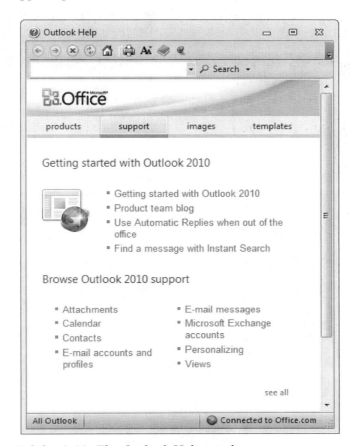

Exhibit 1-11: The Outlook Help window

To search for help on a particular topic, enter a term or phrase in the search box, and then press Enter or click Search. The Outlook Help window also contains links to various guides, blogs, and other support content. Some of that information is located on the Office.com Web site; you must have an Internet connection to access that information.

C-1: Getting help

Here's how	Here's why
1 Click 🔘	(In the upper-right corner of the Outlook window.) To open the Outlook Help window.
2 Click in the search box as indicated	
Type **Calendar**	Case doesn't matter.
Press (↵ ENTER)	After a moment, topics related to the Calendar are displayed.
3 Click a help topic	To display information on the selected topic.
4 Beside the Search button, click the arrow	To display options for controlling where Outlook searches for related information.
Press (ESC)	To close the menu.
5 Close the Outlook Help window	Click its Close button.
6 Press (F1)	In addition to clicking the Help button, you can press the F1 key to open the Outlook Help window.
7 Close the Outlook Help window	Click its Close button.

Students might have to wait for some time to see the results.

Unit summary: Getting started

Topic A   In this topic, you learned how to **start Outlook 2010**. You also learned about the various **window elements**, including the Quick Access toolbar, the Ribbon, the Navigation pane, and the To-Do Bar. Then you learned how to switch from the Mail pane to other panes, such as Calendar, Contacts, and Tasks. Next, you learned how to access the default Outlook folders by using the Folder List pane.

Topic B   In this topic, you learned that **Outlook Today** is a folder that displays your events, appointments, meetings, and tasks planned for the day. You also learned how to **customize** the Calendar, Tasks, and Messages sections of Outlook Today and change the layout of the Outlook Today page.

Topic C   In this topic, you learned how to get help by using the **Outlook Help** window.

Independent practice activity

In this activity, you'll customize the Outlook Today page. You'll also use the Outlook Help window to find information on specific topics.

1 Customize the Outlook Today page to show the following folders in the Messages section: Deleted Items, Inbox, Junk E-mail, Outbox, and Sent Items. (*Hint:* In the Outlook Today pane, click Customize Outlook Today.)

2 Customize the Outlook Today page to be displayed in the Summer style.

3 Save the changes you made in Outlook Today.

4 Close Microsoft Office Outlook 2010.

5 Start Microsoft Office Outlook 2010.

6 Restore the default home page for the Outlook Today page.

   To do so, right-click Student##@outlanderspices.com in the Navigation pane and choose Data File Properties. Click the Home Page tab, click Restore Defaults, and click OK.

7 Click the Help button and then search for help on **Notes**.

8 Look for help topics about **Contacts**.

9 Close the Outlook Help window.

Review questions

1 In addition to sending and receiving e-mail messages, what other activities can you do in Outlook?

You can manage your calendar, maintain contact information, keep track of tasks, and organize notes.

2 Which of the following is not an Outlook item?

A An e-mail message

B A note

C A contact

D The Ribbon

3 Which pane contains the pane-switching buttons that enable you to display the Calendar instead of your Inbox?

The bottom section of the Navigation pane

4 Which default folder would you use to keep a record of interactions that you want to remember?

A Inbox

B Journal

C Sent Items

D Drafts

5 Which default folder stores messages that have been identified as spam?

A Inbox

B Deleted Items

C Junk E-mail

D Drafts

6 True or false? On the Ribbon, the commands available on a tab depend on which view is active.

True. For example, different commands are available on the Home tab depending on whether you're viewing your Inbox or your calendar.

7 Which pane displays the contents of a mail item?

The Reading pane

8 What is Outlook Today?

It is a page that contains a summary of your events, appointments, meetings, and tasks for the day. It also displays the number of messages in the Inbox, Drafts, and Outbox folders.

9 What is the To-Do Bar?

A pane that displays the Date Navigator, your upcoming appointments, and your tasks.

10 Name two ways to open the Outlook Help window.

• *Click the Help (question mark) button.*

• *Press F1.*

Unit 2

E-mail

Unit time: 60 minutes

Complete this unit, and you'll know how to:

A Use the Inbox to preview and read messages.

B Create and send messages, and work with automation and formatting features.

C Reply to messages, forward messages, and delete and restore messages.

D Preview, open, read, forward, and save file attachments, and compress images in attachments.

Topic A: Reading messages

This topic covers the following Microsoft Office Specialist exam objectives for Outlook 2010.

#	Objective
1.2	**Manipulate item tags**
	1.2.1 Categorize items
	1.2.2 Set flags
	1.2.4 Mark items as read or unread

Explanation

You can use Outlook to view, reply to, and forward messages you receive. When you receive an e-mail message, you can save it as a file or forward it to other users. You can also delete e-mail messages and restore deleted messages.

The Inbox

By default, all messages you receive are stored in the *Inbox* folder. This is one of the most frequently used folders in Outlook. You can read messages stored in the Inbox. You can also create and send messages, and reply to messages. The Folder pane displays the Folder Contents list. The Reading pane is used to view messages.

The message header

The header of an e-mail message contains *meta-information*, that is, information about the e-mail message. Header details are shown in the Folder Contents list as well as in the Reading pane. Header details include:

- **Sender** — Tells you who sent the message.
- **Subject** — Indicates the message's subject, if the sender provided this information. This column helps you identify the content of messages.
- **Sending date** — Displays the date and time the message was sent; these are typically close to when you received it.

Messages in the Folder Contents list are marked with various icons that help you identify your Inbox contents at a glance. The following table lists these icons and their meanings:

Objectives 1.2.1, 1.2.2, 1.2.4

Icon	Description	Icon	Description
	A new and unread message		A message with a file attachment
	A message that's been read		A flagged message
	A message that's been read and replied to		A message that's been read and forwarded

Additionally, a category indicator icon is shown for each message. By default, messages are uncategorized, so the box-shaped icon is white. You can assign a category, in which case the icon will be blue, red, or one of the other available colors.

Do it!

A-1: Exploring the Inbox

Here's how	Here's why
1 Select **Inbox**	(In the Navigation pane.) To view your Outlook Inbox.
Click the **Home** tab	If necessary.
2 Observe the commands on the Home tab	It has mail-specific buttons.
3 Observe the status bar	It shows the total number of messages in the Inbox.
4 Examine the e-mail messages	
	Each message shows the name of the sender (Instructor) and the subject of the message. Icons indicate whether you have read the message, the date the message was received, the category you have assigned (if any), and a flag, if you've flagged the message.
5 Select the message with the subject "Welcome to Outlook 2010"	
6 Observe the Reading pane	The Reading pane shows the content of the message that is selected in the Folder Contents list.
Examine the message header	In addition to showing the subject, sender, and date, the Reading pane shows who the message was sent to.

Tell students they might need to widen the Folder Contents list to see the message header.

Previewing and reading messages

Explanation

All new messages are delivered to the Inbox. Messages that have not been read appear in bold with a closed-envelope icon. Messages that have been read appear in regular text with an open-envelope icon.

You can read messages in two ways:

- Previewing
- Reading

Previewing messages

You preview a message by selecting it in the Folder Contents list; the message's contents are then shown in the Reading pane. You can configure the Folder Contents list to show additional data for each message, including its contents. You might enable this option if you were to hide the Reading pane. Otherwise, showing the message's contents in the Folder Contents list would be redundant.

Reading messages

To read a message, you open it in a new window. To do so, double-click the message in the Folder Contents list. Some people prefer to hide the Reading pane and read e-mail messages in a separate window. Doing so provides more screen space for the message, because the Navigation pane and To-Do Bar are not included in the Message window.

As shown in Exhibit 2-1, a Message window contains its own title bar and Ribbon (though not a status bar), as well as sections dedicated to the message header and contents. An additional bar, the People Pane, is present in the Message window, just as it is in the main Outlook window.

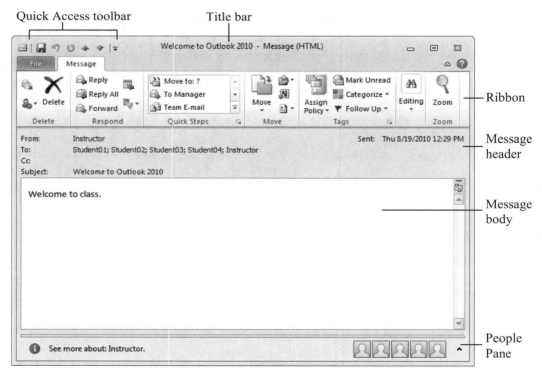

Exhibit 2-1: A received message

Working with the Quick Access toolbar

The Quick Access toolbar contains a selection of commonly used buttons. The default buttons are (from left to right) Save As, Undo, Repeat/Redo, Previous message, Next message, and Customize. You can customize the Quick Access toolbar to include buttons for additional commands.

To the left of the Quick Access toolbar is the Control-menu icon. Click it to display the Control menu, which you can use to close the window or otherwise manipulate the window itself.

Closing the message window

To close a message window, you can do any of the following:

- Click the Control-menu icon and choose Close.
- Click the Close button—the "×" in the window's upper-right corner.
- Press Alt+F4.

Do it!

A-2:   Previewing and reading a message

Here's how	Here's why
1 Select a message	(In the Folder Contents list.) To preview its contents in the Reading pane.
2 Double-click a message	To open the message in a new window.
3 Examine the Ribbon	

	In addition to the Reply, Reply All, and Forward buttons, the Ribbon contains tools for managing messages and junk e-mail and for tracking and editing messages.
4 Close the message window	Click the Close button.

Topic B: Creating and sending messages

This topic covers the following Microsoft Office Specialist exam objectives for Outlook 2010.

#	Objective
2.1	**Create and send e-mail messages**
	2.1.2 Specify message content format
	2.1.2.1 Plain text
	2.1.2.2 Rich text
	2.1.2.3 HTML format
	2.1.3 Show or hide the From and Bcc fields
2.4	**Format item content**
	2.4.1 Use formatting tools
	2.4.5 Use Paste Special

Explanation

E-mail provides a convenient way to communicate with colleagues and friends. To create a message, click the New E-mail button on the Home tab. A blank untitled Message window opens, as shown in Exhibit 2-2.

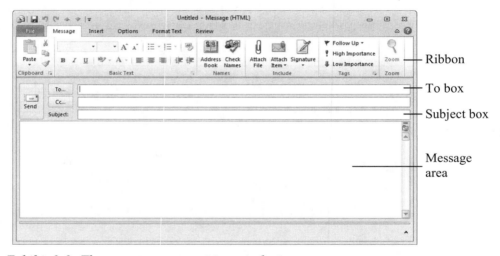

Exhibit 2-2: The message composition window

The following table describes the components of a new Message window.

Component	Used to...
To box	Enter the e-mail addresses of all the people to whom you want to send the message. To send a message to multiple recipients, separate the e-mail addresses with semicolons.
Cc box	Enter the e-mail addresses of all the people to whom you want to send a copy of the message. Officially, cc stands for "carbon copy," a holdover from the days of the typewriter and carbon paper. A more modern interpretation might be "courtesy copy."
Subject box	Type a word or phrase that describes the message.
Message area	Type your message.
Ribbon	Perform various actions, such as sending messages, attaching files, and flagging messages. You can also use buttons here to apply styles, fonts, and other formatting to your message text.

The Bcc box

Objective 2.1.3

Recipients can see who a message is sent to by looking at the e-mail header in their Outlook window. This is also true when you include a recipient on the cc line. However, you can send a "blind carbon copy" (bcc) to a recipient. He or she will receive the copy, but none of the other recipients will see his or her name on the To or Cc lines.

By default, a new message window does not include a Bcc box. To add the Bcc box to a message you're composing, click the Options tab on the Ribbon, and in the Fields group, click Show Bcc.

Selecting the message format

Objectives 2.1.2, 2.1.2.1–2.1.2.3

By default, new messages are composed in HTML format. HTML formatting in a message enables you to apply character and paragraph formats to your message's body text (not to its subject line). You can also compose messages as plain text or Rich Text.

Plain-text messages cannot contain any formatting, such as bold or italics. However, plain-text messages are the smallest in size and most universally supported across various computer platforms and e-mail programs. Rich Text formatting is compatible only with Outlook and Exchange. If you use Rich Text and send a message to someone using an e-mail client other than Outlook, the formatting will be lost.

To change the message format for a single message, create the message and click the Format Text tab. Then click Plain Text or Rich Text in the Format group.

To change the default message format for all messages, click the File tab and then click Options. In the left pane of the Outlook Options dialog box, click Mail. From the "Compose messages in this format" list, select the default format you want to use. Click OK.

Sending messages

You can send your message by clicking the Send button on the Ribbon or by pressing Ctrl+Enter. When you do either, the message is transferred to your Outbox folder. Outlook periodically delivers e-mail and downloads new messages. To force Outlook to send and receive e-mail, click Send/Receive All Folders on the Send/Receive tab.

Whenever you are online and receive a new message, a Desktop Alert appears in the notification area on the Windows taskbar.

Do it!

Objectives 2.1.2, 2.1.3

⚠ *Assign each student a partner. Make sure students know their partner's number.*

B-1: Creating and sending a message

Here's how	Here's why
1 Verify that the Inbox is active	
2 Click **New E-mail**	To create a message.
3 In the To box, enter **Student##**	In place of ##, enter your partner's number.
4 Press (TAB)	To move the insertion point to the Cc box. You can enter another e-mail address here to send a copy of the message to that person.
5 In the Cc box, enter your instructor's e-mail address	
6 Click the **Options** tab and observe the Show Fields group	You can use these options to insert the Bcc and From boxes.
Click **Bcc** and observe the message	The Bcc box appears under the Cc box.
7 Click the **Bcc** button again	To hide the Bcc box.
8 In the Subject box, enter **Greetings classmate**	
9 In the message area, enter **This is a message from your classmate.**	
10 Click the **Format Text** tab	
Observe the Format group	You can use these options to send the message in HTML, plain text, or Rich Text format. The default is HTML.

Tell students that a message might appear, stating that they have received a new message.

11 Be prepared to watch the Outbox folder, which is located roughly in the middle of the Navigation pane

Click **Send** (To the left of the To, Cc, and Subject boxes.) To send the message.

Students should not have to click Send/Receive. If they do, it's on the Send/Retrieve tab.

Observe the Outbox folder Briefly, a "[1]" should appear after the folder's name. Outlook then transmits your message, removing it from the Outbox.

12 Observe the message from your partner

◢ Today		
✉ **student11**	10:22 AM	⬜ ⚑
Greetings classmate		

It will appear in your Inbox.

Select the message To preview it in the Reading pane.

Automation features

Explanation

Microsoft Outlook includes various automation features that help you more easily manage your communications. These include:

- Address lookup and completion
- Word editor integration

Address lookup and completion

When you manually enter names in the To and Cc boxes, Outlook automatically checks your address books for the names. Address books contain the names of people with whom you frequently communicate. If the name you're entering is one you've previously used, Outlook will suggest the matching name or names.

You can either continue typing the name or select it from the shortcut menu. Pressing Tab or Enter will select the first name in the list. You can also press Ctrl+K or click Check Names (on the Ribbon) to look up matching names in your address book, even those names to whom you haven't sent messages recently. Outlook displays the results in a dialog box; double-click a name to enter it in the To or Cc box.

Word editor integration

By default, Outlook uses Microsoft Word components within the message composition window. It's as if the message-body box were a mini Word document. This enables you to take advantage of Word's editing features, such as AutoCorrect, AutoComplete, inline spelling and grammar correction, and more. For example, as you type, Outlook (using Word components) automatically checks the spelling of your text. You'll see the same red, wavy underlines beneath misspelled words that you do when typing a report. You can use also Word's AutoComplete features to ease the entry of common items, such as dates.

Do it!

B-2: Working with automation features

Here's how	Here's why
1 Open a new Message window	Click New E-mail.
2 In the To box, enter **S**	A list appears, showing the names, starting with S, to whom you have recently sent e-mail.
Press `TAB`	Outlook automatically completes the name based on the e-mail address that you used earlier. Notice that Student## is entered in the box automatically.
In the Subject box, enter **Testing Outlook automation**	
3 Press `TAB`	To move the insertion point into the message area.
4 Type **today**	
Press `SPACEBAR`	Notice that the "today" you typed is converted to "Today" because of Word's AutoCorrect feature.

5 Type **is** and press SPACEBAR

Type the first four letters of today's weekday

Subject:	Testing O
Tuesday (Press ENTER to Insert)	
Today is tues	

For example, type "tues" if today is Tuesday.

Press ↵ ENTER

To complete the word automatically.

6 Type **,**

Subject:	Testing Outlook automa
Tuesday, February 09, 2010 (Press ENTER to Insert)	
Today is Tuesday,	

(A comma.) Outlook displays the full date.

Press ↵ ENTER

To complete the full date.

7 Type a period, and then press ↵ ENTER twice

To complete the sentence and start a new paragraph.

8 Type **I'm lerning Outlook.**

I'm lerning Outlook.

A red, wavy underline indicates that "lerning" is misspelled.

9 Right-click **lerning**

learning

leaning

kerning

leering

Ignore

A shortcut menu and the Mini toolbar appear. The shortcut menu displays possible corrections for the misspelled word.

Choose **learning**

To correct the misspelled word.

10 Click **Send**

To send the message to your partner.

Formatting messages

Explanation

Objective 2.4.1

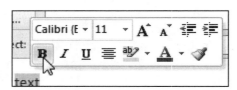

When you create or reply to a message, you might want to emphasize some important text. You can do this by changing its color, size, or font or by applying underlining or italics. You can use the Basic Text group on the Ribbon's Message tab, shown in Exhibit 2-3, to format the text in a message.

Exhibit 2-3: The Message tab on the Ribbon in a new Message window

For additional styles and formatting options, use the Format Text tab, shown in Exhibit 2-4.

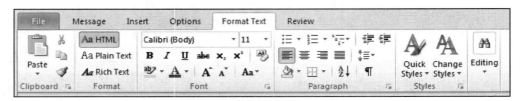

Exhibit 2-4: The Format Text tab

You can also use the Mini toolbar to format the text in a message. When you select the text you want to format, the Mini toolbar appears above the selected text, as shown in Exhibit 2-5. If you point away from the selected text, the Mini toolbar will disappear.

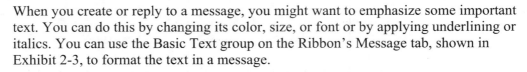

Exhibit 2-5: The Mini toolbar

Do it!

Objective 2.4.1

B-3:   Formatting a message

Here's how	Here's why
1 Open a new Message window	Click New E-mail.
2 In the To box, enter the name of your partner	To address the message to your partner.
In the Subject box, enter **Venue for the class**	
Press TAB	To move the insertion point into the message area.
In the message area, type as shown (including the misspelling)	The venu for today's class is: Outlander Spices, 1170 Blackhorse Ave, Texas
3 Select the first line of text, as shown	The venu for today's class is: You'll format this text.
4 From the Font Size list, select **12**	The list is in the Basic Text group on the Message tab.
From the Font list, select **Arial Black**	
Deselect the text	(Click anywhere in the message area.) The font and size of the message text have changed.
5 Select **Outlander Spices** and click **B**	(The Bold button is on the Ribbon.) To make the selected text bold.
Deselect the text, and click at the end of the text	To see the changes and place the insertion point at the end of the text.
6 Press ↵ ENTER	
Type **Time:** and press SPACEBAR	
Type **10:30 AM tomorrow**	To specify the time of the class.
7 Double-click **tomorrow** but don't move the mouse pointer afterward	The Mini toolbar appears as a semi-transparent pop-up.
Point to the Mini toolbar	It changes from semi-transparent to fully visible.
From the Font Size list, select **14**	On the Mini toolbar.
8 Deselect the text	If necessary.

Tell students they will use the spelling checker in a later activity.

Checking spelling and grammar in messages

Explanation

By default, Microsoft Word checks spelling and grammar automatically as you type. If you misspell a word, a wavy red line appears under the word. If Word finds a grammatical problem, a wavy green line appears under the word or words. If you mistype a word and the result is not a misspelling (for example, "form" instead of "from"), the spelling checker will not flag the word.

You can postpone proofing your message until after you finish writing it. To start checking the spelling, click the Review tab and then click Spelling & Grammar in the Proofing group, or press F7. The same Spelling and Grammar dialog box you would see in Word is opened, as shown in Exhibit 2-6. (The language your system is configured to use will be displayed after the dialog box's name. In the exhibit, U.S. English is the default language.)

The language indicator will differ if you're using a language other than U.S. English.

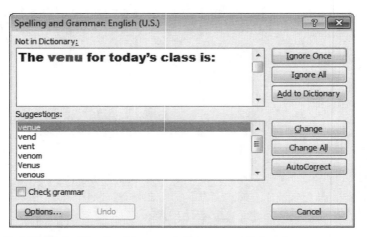

Exhibit 2-6: The Spelling and Grammar dialog box

The misspelled word is shown in the Not in Dictionary box, and suggestions are shown in the Suggestions list. Select the appropriately spelled word and click Change to change a single occurrence of the misspelled word, or click Change All to change all occurrences of that word. You can also click Ignore Once to ignore one instance or click Ignore All to ignore all instances of a specific word.

Do it!

B-4:   Checking a message's spelling

Here's how	Here's why
1 Click the **Review** tab	
2 Click the indicated button	 **ABC** ✓ Spelling & Grammar To open the Spelling and Grammar dialog box. This dialog box opens only when there is an incorrect word in the message.
3 Observe the Spelling and Grammar dialog box	It displays the incorrect word ("venu") in red and prompts you to correct it by selecting a word from the Suggestions list.
From the Suggestions list, select **venue**	(If necessary.) This is the correct spelling.
4 Click **Change**	A message box appears, informing you that the spelling and grammar check is complete.
Click **OK**	To close the message box. Notice that "Venu" has changed to "Venue."
5 Send the message	
6 Check for new messages	If necessary, click Send/Receive.
7 Select the message with the subject **Venue for the class**	(Click the message in the Inbox.) The contents of the message appear in the Reading pane. The message includes the formatting your partner applied.

TIPS *Tell students that they can also press F7.*

Mention that there might be additional spelling mistakes if the message was not typed correctly.

Paste options

Explanation

Objective 2.4.5

The various applications in Office 2010 provide you with a number of ways to paste content into a document, and Outlook 2010 is no exception. When you click the Paste button's arrow, you're presented with a Paste Options menu, as shown in Exhibit 2-7. The paste options will vary, depending on what text you've cut or copied to the Clipboard. When you point to each option, you'll see an example of what its result will look like in the message body.

Exhibit 2-7: Paste options

The typical paste options are described in the following table.

Option	Name and description
	Use Destination Theme — Uses the theme, including fonts, defined for your e-mail messages. This option will format the pasted content so it looks like the current message text.
	Keep Source Formatting — Keeps the formatting used in the document from which you copied the content. When you choose this option, the content will look like it did in the original document or Web page.
	Merge Formatting — Outlook will incorporate both the source and the message format.
	Keep Text Only — Only the text will be pasted; the text will not be formatted.
Paste Special...	Paste Special — Opens the Paste Special dialog box, shown in Exhibit 2-8. You can use this dialog box to paste text as any of the following:

- A Microsoft Office object, whose content you can edit by using the original Office application, such as Word or Excel

- Formatted text (RTF)

- Plain text only

- HTML

- Unformatted Unicode Text, which is a text-only format

You can also paste the item as a link to the original document, using any of the formats described above. A link between the source and the message content will allow you to update the message content if any changes are made in the same content in the source (for example, text in a Word document or numbers in an Excel spreadsheet are changed).

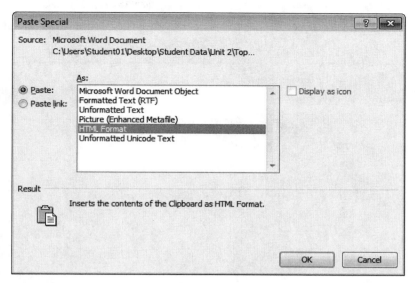

Exhibit 2-8: Paste Special options

B-5: Pasting content from an Office document

The files for this activity are in Student Data folder **Unit 2\Topic B**.

Here's how	Here's why
1 Create a message and address it to your partner	
Type the subject **Sales for Last Two Quarters**	
2 In the message area, type **Here's a quick summary.**	
Press ⏎ ENTER twice	To create line breaks.
3 From Windows Explorer, open Analysis	To open the source document in Word.
Select **Sales Analysis...** and the table beneath it	
Click 📋	(The Copy button.) To copy the text.
Close Word	
4 Switch to Outlook	If necessary.
Click the Paste button's arrow	To display the paste options.
5 Point to 📋	(Use Destination Theme.) To see what the text would look like using the current theme in Outlook.
6 Point to 📋	(Keep Source Formatting.) To see the text using the formatting from the Word document.
7 Point to 📋	(Merge Formatting.) To see the text with both Outlook and Word formatting merged.
8 Point to 📋	(Keep Text Only.) To show the text only, without any formatting. The table is broken.
9 Choose **Paste Special...**	To open the Paste Special dialog box. You can paste the text or a link to the source text in the Word document.
Select **Microsoft Word Document Object** and click **OK**	

10 Double-click the table in the Outlook message body	To open the text for editing in Word. The Paste Special option you chose allows you to open the text in the original application if you want to change it before you send the message.
11 Close Word and send the message	
Close Windows Explorer	If necessary.

Topic C: Working with messages

This topic covers the following Microsoft Office Specialist exam objectives for Outlook 2010.

#	Objective
2.3	**Create item content**
	2.3.2 Insert a hyperlink
3.1	**Clean up the mailbox**
	3.4.4 Specify options for forwards

Explanation

Outlook provides a variety of tools for managing your e-mail messages. Using Outlook, you can:

- Reply to messages
- Forward messages
- Delete and restore e-mail messages

Replying to messages

When you open a received message, Outlook provides two reply buttons in the Respond group on the Ribbon:

- **Reply** — Creates a return message addressed only to the sender.
- **Reply All** — Creates a return message addressed to the sender and everyone who received a carbon copy of the original message.

Reply messages, by default, contain the original message text. This is useful when you need to refer to the original message. Also, when you type any text in the reply Message window, the text appears in blue so you can distinguish between your reply and the original message text.

E-mail etiquette suggests that you should trim the original message text to just the pertinent portions. Many people consider it rude to include screen after screen of prior text in a reply.

To send a reply:

1 Preview or open the message to which you want to reply.
2 Click Reply. This opens the reply Message window, with the name of the original sender in the To box. The reply message uses the subject of the original message with "RE:" added as a prefix.
3 Type your reply in the message area.
4 Click Send.

Do it!

C-1: Replying to a message

Here's how	Here's why
1 Select the message with the subject **Greetings classmate**	(Click the message in your Inbox.) You'll reply to this message.
2 Click **Reply**	To open a reply Message window and compose a reply.
Observe the reply Message window	*[Message window showing To... student11, Cc..., Subject: RE: Greetings classmate, Send button]* The To box contains the name of the message sender. The Subject box displays the same subject, but with RE: added as a prefix.
3 Verify that the insertion point is in the first line of the message area	You'll type your reply here.
4 Type **Thank you**	
Press ⏎ ENTER	The message text is blue.
5 Move to the next line	Press Enter.
Type your name	
6 Send the message	Click Send.
7 Click as shown	*[student11 10:22 AM / Greetings classmate]*
8 Observe the message in the Reading pane	**Greetings classmate** / student11 / ⓘ You replied to this message on 4/27/2010 10:42 AM. / The message indicates the action taken on the message, along with the date and time. In this case, the action was replying to a message.
9 Observe the Folder Contents list	*[Student02]* / The original message now has an icon showing that you have replied to the message.
10 In the Navigation pane, click **Sent Items**	To open the Sent Items folder. The reply you sent appears here. Any message you send will be stored in this folder.
11 Select your Inbox	Next, you'll use the Reply All option.

Tell students that the name might differ.

Help students identify the icon.

	12 Select the message with the subject **Greetings classmate**	You'll send a reply to the sender and to anyone who received a Cc.
	13 Click **Reply All**	To open a reply Message window.
The Cc line should include the Instructor.	14 Observe the Reply message window	The To box contains the name of the sender of the message, and the Cc box contains the name of the person who received a copy of the original message. (In this case, Instructor should be listed on the Cc line.)
	15 Type **Hello!**	In the message area.
	16 Click **Send**	To send the reply to the sender and to the person who was copied on the original message.

Forwarding messages

Explanation

Objective 3.4.4

When you receive a message that other people need to know about, you can forward it to them. To forward a message:

1 Open or select the message.

2 Click Forward.

3 Enter the recipient's name in the To box.

4 Click Send.

By default, when you forward a message, you're really creating a new message. And in that new message, the entire original message is included in the body text, with the insertion point at the top of the new message, above the original message text. You can change this default behavior by using the Outlook Options dialog box.

To open the dialog box, click the File tab and then click Options. In the left pane, click Mail to display the mail properties that you can configure. Scroll to find the "Replies and forwards" section, shown in Exhibit 2-9. Using these settings, you can configure the following forwarding options:

- Close the original message window after you click Forward. This can help you clean up the desktop by closing an unnecessary window.

- Insert your name before your comments if you make any comments inside the original message text.

- Configure the appearance of the original message text in the body of your forwarded message.

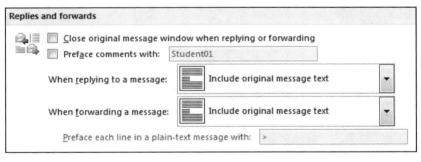

Exhibit 2-9: Forwarding options

Do it!

C-2: Forwarding a message

Here's how	Here's why
1 Click the **File** tab and then click **Options**	To open the Outlook Options dialog box.
2 In the left pane, click **Mail** Scroll to the "Replies and forwards" section	
3 Observe the settings	You can configure Outlook to close the original message window when you click Forward, preface your inline comments with your user name, and configure how original message text appears in your forwarded message.
Click **Cancel**	
4 Select the message with the subject **Venue for the class**	In the Inbox Folder Contents list.
5 Click [Forward icon]	The message opens in a new Message window. The subject of the message is the original subject, with the prefix FW: added.
6 In the To box, enter **Student*XX***	(Where *XX* is the number of a classmate other than your partner.) To forward the message to the specified user.
7 In the message area, type **I thought you might find this useful.**	Notice that the text you type appears in blue.
8 Send the message	
9 Open the Sent Items folder	(Click Sent Items in the Mail pane.) The message you forwarded appears in the Sent Items Folder Contents list.

Objective 3.4.4

TIPS *Tell students they can also right-click the message and choose Forward.*

⚠ *Make sure students don't enter Administrator, their partner's user name, or Instructor.*

Hyperlinks

Explanation

Objective 2.3.2

Sharing favorite or useful Web sites is a common use of e-mail. You might send friends links to sites you think are funny or informative, or send colleagues links to sites providing valuable information for projects or day-to-day operations. Sharing a hyperlink is as easy as performing a copy and paste.

First, in your Web browser, select the text in the Address bar. Either press Ctrl+C, or right-click the selected text and choose Copy. Then, in Outlook, create a message and address it to your intended recipients. When you get to the body of the message, click the Paste button's arrow and choose the Keep Text Only option.

You can also insert a hyperlink from within Outlook by using the Insert Hyperlink dialog box, shown in Exhibit 2-10. This dialog box offers several options not available when you just copy and paste a hyperlink.

- You can label the hyperlink with a title and create a custom ScreenTip for it.
- You can create a link to a file, a Web page, a location within a file or Web page, or an e-mail address.

To open the Insert Hyperlink dialog box, click the Insert tab and then click Hyperlink in the Links group. Or you can right-click a blank area of a message and choose Hyperlink.

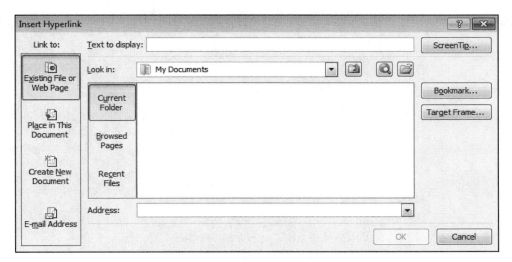

Exhibit 2-10: Inserting a hyperlink

Do it!

Objective 2.3.2

C-3:   Inserting a hyperlink

Here's how	Here's why
1 Open Internet Explorer and navigate to **www.microsoft.com\outlook**	
	To visit a Web page that you'll link to in an e-mail message.
If prompted to set up Internet Explorer, close the dialog box	

2 Click in the Address bar	`http://office.microsoft.com/en-us/outlook`
	To select the text. You'll see the address changed to the correct address for Microsoft's Outlook home page.
Right-click the selected text and choose **Copy**	
3 In Outlook, click **New E-Mail**	On the Home tab.
In the To box, enter your partner's e-mail address	
In the Subject box, type **Interesting Outlook information**	
4 Right-click in the message body, and under Paste Options, click **Keep Text Only**	To paste the hyperlink into the new message.
5 Press ⏎ ENTER twice	To create two blank lines.
6 Click the **Insert** tab, and in the Links group, click 🔗 Hyperlink	To open the Insert Hyperlink dialog box.
7 Observe the dialog box	In the Link to list, you can select what you want to link to, including a file or Web page, a place in a document you're working on, a new document, or an e-mail address. You can use the "Text to display" box to label the hyperlink, and use the ScreenTip button to create a ScreenTip.
8 In the Link to list, verify that **Existing File or Web Page** is selected	
In the details pane, click **Browsed Pages**	
Select the **Microsoft Outlook 2010** link	The "Text to display" box contains the page's title. The Address box contains the Web address of the page you visited earlier in this task.
9 Click **OK**	To close the Insert Hyperlink dialog box.
Observe the link	It has the title you saw in the "Text to display" box. If you compare it to the link you copied into the message, you can see that it looks a little more professional than a plain Web address.
10 Click **Send**	To send the message to your partner.

Deleting and restoring messages

Explanation

Objective 3.1

You can delete messages that you don't need any longer. To delete a message, you select it and then either click the Delete button (on the Home tab) or press the Delete key.

Deleted messages are not immediately removed. Instead, they are moved to the Deleted Items folder. This means you can recover accidentally deleted items by moving them out of the Deleted Items folder into another folder. You can also select a message, click the Home tab, click Move (in the Move group), and choose Other Folder. In the Move Items dialog box, select the folder you want to move the message to and click OK.

To permanently delete an item, you must empty the Deleted Items folder. To do so, select that folder, click the Folder tab, and click Empty Folder. You can also right-click the Deleted Items folder and choose Empty Folder.

If you're using a Microsoft Exchange Server account, messages might still be recoverable even after you empty the Deleted Items folder. Click the Folder tab and then click Recover Deleted Items. Select the messages you want to recover, and click the Recover Selected Items button, which is the enveloped-shaped button, second from the left. The messages will appear in the Deleted Items folder. The Exchange administrator controls how long deleted messages will be recoverable.

Do it!

Objective 3.1

C-4: Deleting and restoring a message

Here's how	Here's why
1 Open the Inbox folder	Click Inbox in the Mail pane.
2 Select the message with the subject **Your second message**	You'll delete this message.
3 Click ✖ Delete	(On the Home tab.) To delete the message. It is removed from the Folder Contents list.
4 Select the Instructor's message with the subject **Welcome to Outlook 2010**	
Press DELETE	To delete the message.
5 Open the Deleted Items folder	(Click Deleted Items in the Mail pane.) The deleted messages appear in this folder, which stores all of the deleted messages.
6 Drag the **Welcome to Outlook 2010** message to the Inbox folder in the Mail pane	To restore the deleted message.
Select the **Inbox** folder	The message has been restored to your Inbox.
7 Select the **Deleted Items** folder	
Click the **Folder** tab	
Click **Empty Folder**	To remove the message from the Deleted Items folder. A message box prompts you to confirm the deletion.
Click **Yes**	The folder is emptied.
8 Click **Recover Deleted Items**	On the Folder tab.
Select the message with the subject **Your second message**	
Click 🖳	After a moment or two, the message appears in the Deleted Items folder again.

Tell students that the Recover Deleted Items command is available only when a Microsoft Exchange account is used.

If the message doesn't appear at first, have the students wait a moment or close the window and try again.

9 Click the **File** tab and then click **Options**	To open the Outlook Options dialog box. You'll configure Outlook to automatically delete items from your Deleted Items folder when you close Outlook.
Click **Advanced**	
In the "Outlook start and exit" section, check **Empty Deleted Items folders when exiting Outlook**	
Click **OK**	To close the Outlook Options dialog box.

Topic D: Handling attachments

This topic covers the following Microsoft Office Specialist exam objectives for Outlook 2010.

#	Objective
2.3	**Create item content**
	2.3.1 Insert graphical elements
2.5	**Attach content to e-mail messages**
	2.5.2 Attach external files
3.1	**Clean up the mailbox**
	3.1.2 Save message attachments

Explanation

In addition to sending a standard e-mail message, you can add an attachment to the message. When you receive an e-mail message that includes an attachment, you can preview or save the attachment. You can also forward the attachment to others.

Attach a file to a new message

Objective 2.5.2

You can attach any type of file to an e-mail message in order to send the file to the recipient. For example, you can send Word, graphics, sound, and movie files as attachments. You can attach a single file or multiple files to a message. The Attached box displays the name and size of each attachment.

To attach a file:

1   Create a message.
2   Click the Attach File button in the Include group on the Ribbon.
3   Select the file you want to insert, and click Insert. The Attached box, listing the attached file, appears under the Subject box.

By default, Outlook blocks potentially unsafe attachments, such as EXE and VBS files, which can contain viruses. If you attach a file with an extension that might be blocked by Outlook, you will be asked whether you want to send a potentially unsafe attachment. If you send the attachment anyway, it might be blocked by the recipient's Outlook program or antivirus software.

Forward a message that contains an attachment

You can forward a message that contains an attachment by opening the message and clicking Forward. By default, the file is attached to the message. Type your note, address the message, and click Send.

You can also forward a message and add an attachment. To do so:

1   Open the message you want to forward.
2   Click the Forward button in the Respond group on the Ribbon.
3   Click the Attach File button in the Include group on the Ribbon.
4   Select the file you want to insert, and click Insert. The Attached box, listing the attached file, appears under the Subject box.

Do it!

D-1: Sending and forwarding attachments

The files for this activity are in Student Data folder **Unit 2\Topic D**.

Objective 2.5.2

Here's how	Here's why
1 Click the **Home** tab	
2 Click **New E-mail**	
Address the message to your partner	In the To box, type your partner's e-mail address.
Enter the subject as **Sales Report**	
3 In the message area, type **I am sending the West Coast sales report.**	
4 Click Attach File	(In the Include group on the Ribbon.) To open the Insert File dialog box.
5 Navigate to the current topic folder	Student Data folder Unit 2\Topic D.
Select **Analysis**	(If necessary.) Analysis is a Word document that contains a table and a graph showing the growth of sales.
Click **Insert**	 To attach the file. The Attached box appears under the Subject box and displays the name and size of the attachment.
6 Send the message	After a moment, your partner's message will appear in your Inbox. If it doesn't, click Send/Receive on the Send/Receive tab.
7 Observe the new message in your Inbox	 The attachment icon (a paperclip) appears to the right of the subject in the header information.

Help students locate the current topic folder.

Tell students that the user name might differ.

8 Select the message from your partner	
9 Click **Forward**	The attachment appears in the Attached field.
10 Click [×]	To close the message without sending it.

Students might notice file size differences. These are caused by the way the file is encoded and attached to the message.

Resizing images and image attachments

Explanation

Objectives 2.3.1, 2.5.2

If you are using HTML or the Rich Text format for your messages, you can insert images into the message body or as attachments. If you insert or attach large pictures or several pictures, you might want to resize them to make the message smaller.

Inserting vs. attaching

When you insert an image, it appears within the text of your message, much like a picture you insert in a Word memo appears within the document. An attached image is treated just like an attached document: it is listed in the Attached box when you send the message, and it is not displayed inline.

Resizing image attachments

You can use an image editing program to resize an image before attaching it to your e-mail message. However, Outlook can handle the task for you automatically.

After attaching the image, click the File tab. If necessary, click Info. Then select "Resize large images when I send this message." Outlook will automatically resize the image to a maximum of 1024 × 768 pixels.

Compressing inserted images

After you insert pictures into a message, select an image to display the Picture Tools | Format tab. (This is one of Outlook's *contextual tabs*—tabs that appear only in certain circumstances.) Click the Compress Pictures button, select a compression option, and click OK.

Do it!

Objectives 2.3.1, 2.5.2

D-2: Inserting, attaching, and compressing images

The files for this activity are in Student Data folder **Unit 2\Topic D**.

Here's how	Here's why
1 Create a message	
2 In the To box, enter the name of your partner	
3 In the Subject box, enter **Spice Picture 1**	
In the message area, type **Here's the first spice arrangement picture for the newsletter.**	
4 Click **Attach File**	The Attach File button is in the Include group on the Ribbon.
5 Navigate to the current topic folder	
Point to Spicearrangement1	The image is an approximately 1.3 MB TIF file.
Select **Spicearrangement1**	
Click **Insert**	
6 In the Message window, click the **File** tab	The Info command will be selected by default.
Select **Resize large images when I send this message**	

Image Attachments

Some recipients may not receive this message because of image attachments. Resizing large images may help the message get delivered. Resized images will be a maximum of 1024x768 pixels.

◉ Resize large images when I send this message.
◯ Do not resize images.

Click the **Message** tab	
7 Click **Send**	The image is resized automatically and the message is delivered.
8 Create a message addressed to your partner	
9 In the Subject box, enter **Spice Picture 2**	

10 In the message area, type
**Here's the second
arrangement picture.**

Press (↵ ENTER)

11 Click the **Insert** tab

Click **Picture**

Navigate to the current topic folder

Select
Spicearrangement2.tif   The size of the file is approximately 1.3 MB.

Click **Insert**   To insert the picture in the body of the message. The Picture Tools | Format tab appears.

12 Click [icon]   The Compress Picture button is in the Adjust group on the Picture Tools | Format tab.

Under Target output, select
**E-mail (96 ppi): minimize
document size for sharing**   To optimize the picture in the message to a size suitable for e-mailing.

Click **OK**

13 Click **Send**   Your partner's messages will arrive in your Inbox in a few moments. Click Send/Receive if they do not.

14 Select the **Spice Picture 1** message

> ✉ Message | 🖼 Spicearrangment1.jpg (140 KB)

Notice that the attachment is a JPG file instead of a TIF file, and it is considerably smaller than 1.3 MB.

Tell students that the size might be slightly different from that shown.

15 In the Inbox Folder Contents list, point to the Spice Picture 2 message

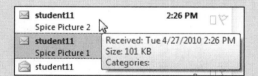

The message is just over 100 KB, much smaller than the original image.

Previewing and saving attachments

Explanation

When you receive a message containing a file attachment, the message will have a paperclip icon in the Folder Contents list. The icon appears to the left of the sender's name (as part of the header information). You can view the name and size of the attachment, as shown in Exhibit 2-11, in the header of the Reading pane or in the opened message.

Exhibit 2-11: An attachment

Previewing or opening an attachment

When a message contains an attachment, you can click the attachment's name to preview the file in the Reading pane or message window. You can open the attachment in its associated program by double-clicking the attachment's name. For example, double-clicking a Word document opens Microsoft Word.

Saving an attachment

Objective 3.1.2

You can save all attachments or a single attachment to an e-mail message. There are several ways to save an attachment:

- Use the Save As button on the Attachments tab.
- Right-click the attachment and choose Save As.
- Double-click the attachment, and once the attachment is opened in its associated program, save it from within that program.

Do it!

Objective 3.1.2

D-3:   Previewing and saving an attachment

Here's how	Here's why
1 Select the **Sales Report** message from your partner	To display the message contents in the Reading pane.
2 In the Reading pane, observe the attachment area	✉ Message | 📄 Analysis.docx (20 KB) It displays a Message button and the name and size of the attachment.
3 In the Reading pane, click the attachment's file name	You'll see the message "Starting Microsoft Word Previewer" in the Reading pane. After a moment, the attachment is displayed inline.
In the Folder Contents list, click the message	To display the message again without previewing the attachment.
4 Double-click the attachment's file name	To open the attachment in Microsoft Word. The Opening Mail Attachment dialog box might appear.
5 Close Microsoft Word	To return to Outlook.
6 In the Reading pane, select the attachment	
7 On the Attachments tab, in the Actions group, click **Save As**	
8 Navigate to the current topic folder	Student Data folder Unit 2\Topic D.
Edit the File name box to read **My sales**	To save the attachment with a different name.
Click **Save**	To save the attachment and close the Save As dialog box.
9 Select the **Spice Picture 2** message	(In the Folder Contents list.) The image that your partner inserted into that message is immediately visible. It's not an attachment.
10 Right-click the picture	The shortcut menu includes the Save As Picture command. You could click it to save this picture, just like you saved the attachment.
Press (ESC)	To close the shortcut menu.

⚠ *If students double-click, Word will open.*

Tell students that because Word is installed on their computers, they can preview the attachment.

Tell students that usually they would not change the file name. They're doing so now because there's already a file by that name in the folder.

Unit summary: E-mail

Topic A In this topic, you learned how to work with e-mail messages. You **previewed** a message in the Reading pane and **opened** a message in its own window.

Topic B In this topic, you **created** and **sent** a message. You used automation features such as AutoComplete and Check Names. In addition, you used the Ribbon and the Mini toolbar to format message text. You also learned how to check the **spelling** and **grammar** in a message.

Topic C In this topic, you replied to and forwarded messages. You learned that when replying to a message, you can **reply** to the sender alone or **reply to all** people who received the original message. You also learned how to **delete** messages and **restore** deleted messages from the Deleted Items folder.

Topic D In this topic, you **attached** a file to a message, and you previewed and saved an attachment. Next, you inserted and attached **images** to messages and compressed those images. Then, you previewed, opened, and saved an attachment.

Independent practice activity

In this activity, you'll attach a file to a message, check a message for spelling errors, and save an attached file. You'll also reply to a message and forward a message. You will need to work with a partner to complete this activity.

The files for this activity are in Student Data folder **Unit 2\Unit summary**.

1 Compose a message as shown in Exhibit 2-12. (*Hint:* Enter the name of your mailing partner in the To box and in the message area.)

2 Attach the file **New rules** to the message.

3 Check the message for spelling errors.

4 Send the message to your partner.

5 Read the message you receive from your e-mail partner.

6 Save the attached file with the name **My new rules**.

7 Reply to the e-mail message. In the message area, enter **Thanks for the e-mail. I'll forward a copy to the purchase team.**

8 Forward the message to another student in the class (someone other than your partner).

9 Close the Message window, if necessary.

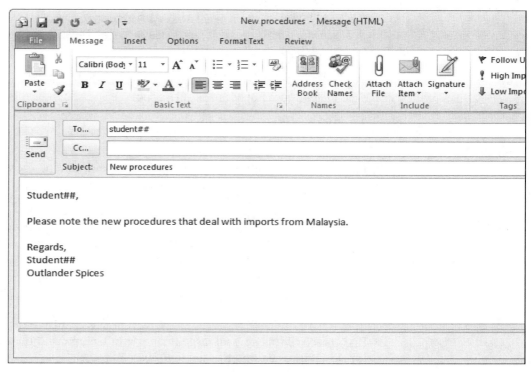

Exhibit 2-12: The Message window with a sample message for Step 1

Review questions

1 When you are looking at the Folder Contents list, what indicates that you've read a particular message?

   An open-envelope icon

2 When should you use the To line versus the Cc line while addressing an e-mail message?

   Use the To line to address a message to someone from whom you expect a response or some sort of action. Use the Cc line to address messages to people who should know of the conversation (they need to stay "in the loop"), but don't need to participate in it.

3 Which feature automatically checks the address book for the message recipient's name?

   A AutoCorrect

   B AutoComplete

   c Name-checking

   D Spell-checking

4 Which feature automatically enters the recipient's name based on e-mail addresses you've used earlier?

   A AutoCorrect

   B AutoComplete

   C Name-checking

   D SmartTags

5 What is the difference between using the Reply button and the Reply All button?

The Reply button creates a return message addressed to only the sender. The Reply All button creates a return message addressed to the sender and to everyone else who received the original message.

6 What is the procedure to attach a file to an e-mail message?

a *Click the Attach File button on the Ribbon.*

b *Select the file you want to insert.*

c *Click Insert.*

7 In what way does a message's subject change when you forward the message?

The letters "FW" appear before the subject text

8 How do you add a Blind Carbon Copy field to a message?

To add the Bcc box to a message you're composing, click the Options tab on the Ribbon, and in the Fields group, click Show Bcc.

9 True or false? An attached image will be displayed inline with the remainder of the e-mail message.

False. The recipient must select the attachment or open it to view it.

10 If you are sending several large images as attachments, how can you resize the images before sending the message?

Attach the files to the message. Then click the File tab and click Info. Select "Resize large images when I send this message." Click the Message tab. Complete and send your message.

Unit 3

E-mail management

Unit time: 50 minutes

Complete this unit, and you'll know how to:

A Set message options such as sensitivity and importance, and set up delivery and read-receipt options for messages.

B Add users to the Blocked Senders and Safe Senders lists, mark messages as Not Junk, and manage junk e-mail options.

C Create and use Search folders to find and organize messages.

D Customize page setup options for printing, and print messages and attachments.

Topic A: Setting message options

This topic covers the following Microsoft Office Specialist exam objectives for Outlook 2010.

#	Objective
1.2	**Manipulate item tags**
	1.2.2 Set flags
	1.2.3 Set sensitivity level
1.3	**Arrange the Content pane**
	1.3.3 Use the Reminders window
2.1	**Create and send e-mail messages**
	2.1.4 Set a reminder for message recipients
	2.1.7 Configure message delivery options
	2.1.9 Configure tracking options
3.4	**Manage automatic message content**
	3.4.3 Specify options for replies

Explanation

When you send an e-mail message, you might want the recipient to know whether it's sensitive (personal or confidential) and whether it's urgent so that he or she can respond accordingly.

Setting the sensitivity level

Objective 1.2.3

You can specify the sensitivity level for an e-mail message. There are four levels of sensitivity: Normal (default), Personal, Private, and Confidential. When you set the sensitivity to a setting other than Normal, a notice indicating the sensitivity level will appear in the recipient's InfoBar.

To set the sensitivity of a message:

1   Create a message.
2   On the Ribbon, click the Dialog Box Launcher in the Tags group, shown in Exhibit 3-1, to open the message Properties dialog box, shown in Exhibit 3-2.
3   Under Settings, select the Sensitivity level you want to use. You can also select an Importance level by using this dialog box.
4   Click Close.
5   Send the message.

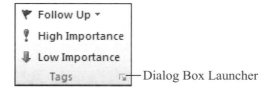
Dialog Box Launcher

Exhibit 3-1: The Dialog Box Launcher in the Tags group

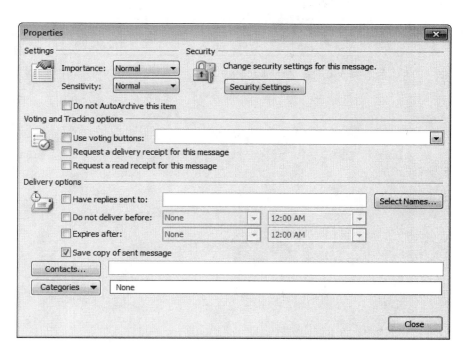

Exhibit 3-2: The message Properties dialog box

Setting the importance level

Use Outlook's importance levels to indicate whether a message is urgent. When you set the importance level for a message to High, a red exclamation mark in the message header tells the recipient that the message needs an immediate response. The default level of importance for a message is Normal. You can also set the importance to Low for messages that don't need a response or that are not a high priority.

To change the importance level for a message, click the High Importance button or the Low Importance button in the Tags group on the Ribbon, as shown in Exhibit 3-1. If neither button is activated, the importance level is set to Normal.

Do it!

A-1:   Defining delivery options

Here's how	Here's why
1 Open a new Message window	(Click New E-mail.) You need to know the time of a team meeting. You'll send a message of high importance to your partner.
Address the message to your partner	
In the Subject box, enter **Meeting time?**	
In the message area, type **Help! I forgot the time of today's team meeting.**	
2 In the Tags group, click [!]	(On the Ribbon.) To set the importance level to High.
3 Click the Dialog Box Launcher, as shown	
	To open the message's Properties dialog box.
4 Under Settings, from the Sensitivity list, select **Private**	Text in the InfoBar will inform the recipient that this e-mail message is private. He or she will not be able to modify it when forwarding or replying to it.
5 Click **Close**	To close the Properties dialog box.
6 Send the message	
7 Observe your Inbox	
	Your partner's message will be listed in your Inbox after a few moments. The red exclamation point indicates that the message was marked as being important.
8 Select the **Meeting time?** message	
	In the Reading pane, the InfoBar informs you that the message is private.

Objective 1.2.3

Tell students they will need to wait for the message from their partner to appear in their Inbox.

9	Click **Reply**	You'll send the time of the team meeting. Notice that the High Importance button is not selected. By default, the importance level resets to Normal when you reply to a message.
	In the message area, type **The meeting is tomorrow at 10:30 AM.**	
	Send the reply	The original message is still selected, and its InfoBar now indicates that you replied.
10	Click **Forward**	You'll forward this message to another person. Notice that the High Importance button is selected. The importance level does not reset to Normal when you forward a message.
11	Click **High Importance**	(In the Tags group.) To remove the High Importance level.
12	Send the message to another student	In the To box, enter the address of a student other than your partner. When the forwarded message is received, no exclamation point appears.

Delaying e-mail delivery

Explanation
You can delay the delivery of an e-mail message. When you do so, the message is not sent until the date and time you specify.

Objective 2.1.7

To delay the delivery of a message:

1 Create a message.

2 Open the message's Properties dialog box by using either of these techniques:

- On the Message tab, in the Tags group, click the Dialog Box Launcher. In the dialog box, check "Do not deliver before."

- On the Options tab, in the More Options group, click Delay Delivery. In the dialog box, "Do not deliver before" is checked automatically.

3 Next to "Do not deliver before," specify the date and time when you want the message to be sent.

4 Click Close.

5 Finish the message and click Send.

Do it!

Objective 2.1.7

A-2: Specifying a delayed e-mail delivery

Here's how	Here's why
1 Open a new Message window	
Address the message to your partner	
In the Subject box, enter **Reminder**	
2 In the message area, type **Don't forget we have a meeting at 10:30.**	The meeting you're referring to is scheduled for tomorrow, so you'll delay the message so it is sent tomorrow.
3 Click the **Options** tab	
4 In the More Options group, click **Delay Delivery**	To open the Properties dialog box. Under Delivery options, "Do not deliver before" is checked.
5 From the list next to "Do not deliver before," select tomorrow's date	
6 From the time list, select **8:00 AM**	To specify the time at which the e-mail message can be sent.
7 Click **Close**	
8 Click **Send**	To send the message. It won't be received until after 8 AM tomorrow.
9 Observe your Outbox folder	(In the Mail pane.) One message is in your Outbox.
Select **Outbox**	To view your Outbox.
Click the **Send/Receive** tab and then click **Send/Receive All Folders**	One item remains in your Outbox. Your scheduled note will remain there until the delivery time you specified.
10 Select **Inbox**	To view your Inbox again.
Click the **Home** tab	

Specifying e-mail reply addresses

Explanation

Objective 3.4.3

By default, when a recipient replies to an e-mail message, the reply is sent to the original sender's address. However, when you send a message, you might want replies to be sent to a different address. For example, if you use more than one e-mail account, you might send a message from one account but want replies to go to another account. Alternately, you might want a response to go to a colleague.

To specify an e-mail address to which replies are sent:

1 Create a message.

2 Open the message's Properties dialog box:

- On the Message tab, in the Tags group, click the Dialog Box Launcher. In the dialog box, check "Have replies sent to."

- On the Options tab, in the More Options group, click Direct Replies To. In the dialog box, "Have replies sent to" is checked automatically.

3 Next to "Have replies sent to," specify the e-mail address to which you want replies sent.

4 Click Close.

5 Finish the message and click Send.

Do it!

Objective 3.4.3

A-3: Specifying an e-mail reply address

Here's how	Here's why
1 Open a new Message window	
Address the message to your partner	
In the Subject box, enter **Out Thursday**	
2 In the message area, type **I'll be out of town Thursday. Contact me in an emergency.**	You'll specify your personal e-mail address for any replies to this message, because while you're out of town, you'll be checking your personal e-mail.
3 Click the **Options** tab	
4 Click **Direct Replies To**	(In the More Options group.) To open the Properties dialog box. Under Delivery options, "Have replies sent to" is checked.
5 Next to "Have replies sent to," enter an alternate e-mail address	Specify an alternate e-mail address provided by your instructor. If no alternate is available, just enter your assigned e-mail address.
6 Click **Close**	
7 Click **Send**	

Tell students which address to use.

Requesting read and delivery receipts

Explanation

Objective 2.1.9

Sometimes it's important to know when a message is delivered to the recipient and when each recipient reads the message. You can track when the messages you sent are delivered and when they are read.

To request notification when a message has been delivered, check "Request a Delivery Receipt" in the Tracking group on the Options tab. When the message is delivered to the user's Inbox, you will receive a message stating that delivery was successful.

To request notification when the message has been read by each recipient, check "Request a Read Receipt" in the Tracking group on the Options tab. When the recipient opens the message, he or she is notified that you've requested a read receipt. The recipient has the option of sending or denying a read receipt. You can identify notification messages in your Inbox by the word "Read:" before the subject.

Do it!

Objective 2.1.9

A-4: Using delivery and read receipts

Here's how	Here's why
1 Create a message and address it to your partner	
Enter the subject **Cinnamon prices in Malaysia**	
In the message area, type **Cinnamon prices doubled today. We'll need to revise our prices.**	
2 Click the **Options** tab	
In the Tracking group, check **Request a Delivery Receipt**	You'll receive a return message with the date and time the message was delivered to the recipient's Inbox.
In the Tracking group, check **Request a Read Receipt**	You'll receive a return message with the date and time when the recipient opens the message.
3 Send the message to your partner	
4 Observe your Inbox	Microsoft Outlook 11:55 AM Delivered: Cinnamon prices in Malaysia
	The icon to the left of the subject indicates that your message was received by your partner. This is your delivery receipt message.
Select the delivery receipt message	(The one with the icon.) In the Reading pane, you'll see a message stating that your e-mail was delivered and listing the recipients.
5 Double-click the **Cinnamon Prices in Malaysia** message	(The message your partner sent you.) To open it. You're prompted to send a read receipt to your partner. (You will not be prompted if you preview the message.)
Click **Yes**	To send the read receipt message.
6 Close the Message window	
7 Observe the read receipt message	student11 11:58 AM Read: Cinnamon prices in Malaysia
	The message with your partner's name is the read receipt. Notice the checkmark icon.
Select the read receipt	In the Reading pane, the message states when your message was read.

Make sure that students don't send the message.

It might take a moment for the messages to show up.

Make sure students select the message with the icon.

It might take a moment for the read receipt to arrive.

Message flags

Explanation

Objectives 1.2.2, 2.1.4

When you receive an e-mail message that you need to follow up on, you can flag it as a reminder. You can also send a flagged message to other people. The message will then alert the recipients that immediate action is needed for that message. Flagged messages create to-do items either for you alone or for you and the recipients of the message.

If your Inbox contains many e-mail messages, you might think it will be difficult to search for flagged messages. However, flagged messages are displayed in the Task list in the To-Do Bar, as shown in Exhibit 3-3.

Exhibit 3-3: Flagged messages in the To-Do Bar's Task list

Sending a flag and reminder with a new message

You can flag a new message and create a reminder for message recipients by using the Follow Up button in the Tags group on the Ribbon. Just click Follow Up and choose Add a Reminder. By default, the message will be flagged for you, and a reminder will be created for a time in the future. Use the Custom dialog box, shown in Exhibit 3-4, to change the reminder time to a time that is appropriate for you.

To flag a message for recipients and create a reminder for them, check Flag for Recipients and specify the date and time you want the reminder to be displayed.

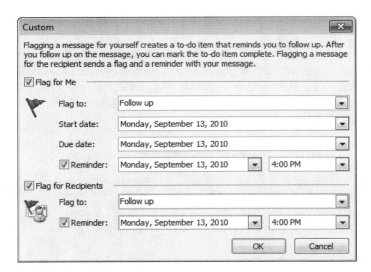

Exhibit 3-4: Creating reminders

Flagging received messages

Flagging a message identifies it for further action by inserting a flag symbol to the right of it in the Folder Contents list. When you flag a received message, you can specify the action to be taken, the due date, and the time.

To flag a message, right-click the flag column to the right of the message and choose one of the menu options shown in Exhibit 3-5. After you set the flag, the InfoBar displays the option you chose. Your flagged message will appear in the To-Do Bar, in Tasks, and in the Daily Task list in the Calendar.

Exhibit 3-5: The Flag menu

Marking a flagged message as completed

After you follow up on a flagged message, you can mark it as completed. You can work with flagged messages in either the To-Do Bar's Task list or the Folder Contents list. To mark a flagged item as complete, either click the message's flag column or right-click the message and choose Mark Complete. The flag changes to a checkmark, and the message is removed from the To-Do Bar's Task list.

Clearing a message flag

If you want to remove the flag from an e-mail message, choose Clear Flag from the Flag menu. When you clear a flag, there is no record of the message ever appearing in views such as the To-Do Bar and Tasks. If you want to keep a record of completed items, use the Mark Complete option.

Do it!

Objectives 1.2.2, 2.1.4

A-5: Flagging an e-mail message

Here's how	Here's why
1 Select the **Cinnamon prices in Malaysia** message	Make sure you select the message sent to you by your partner—it has the envelope icon.
2 Click the flag icon	Cinnamon prices in Malaysia ⬛ 🚩 Student02 2:20 PM To flag the message for follow-up. The message now has a red flag and appears under Today in the To-Do Bar. By default, flagged messages are flagged under Today.
Observe the Reading pane	The InfoBar lists start-by and due-by dates. The default flag marks items as due today.

3	Right-click the flag for the "Cinnamon prices in Malaysia" message	
	Choose **Next Week**	
	Observe the Reading pane	The InfoBar now indicates that you must follow up by the Friday of next week.
4	Right-click the flag for the "Cinnamon prices in Malaysia" message	
	Choose **Mark Complete**	The icon becomes a checkmark.
	Observe the Reading pane	The InfoBar now indicates that you have completed this task.
5	Right-click the checkmark for the "Cinnamon prices in Malaysia" message	
	Choose **Clear Flag**	To remove the flag from the message. The InfoBar message is also removed.
6	Create a message to your partner, with the subject **Price updates**	
7	In the message area, type **Call me today to talk about price changes.**	
8	Click **Follow Up** and choose **Add Reminder...**	To open the Custom dialog box, shown in Exhibit 3-4.
9	Check **Flag for Recipients**, and check **Reminder**	
	Choose today's date, and set the reminder time for 10 minutes from the current time	(Select the numbers in the Time box.) For example, if it's 1:17 p.m., change the time for the reminder to 1:27 p.m.
	Click **OK**	To close the Custom dialog box.
10	Observe the top of the message	(Below the Ribbon.) Your reminder and your recipient's reminder information is displayed.
	Send the message	
11	Observe the new message in your Inbox	

You can have students choose a longer or shorter time. They'll dismiss the reminder in the next activity.

The message has been flagged, and a reminder (indicated by the bell icon) has been created.

The Reminders window

Explanation

The Reminders window is like an alarm clock. It will open on the date and at the time specified in any reminders you have created or have been sent in Outlook. You can use the options in the Reminders window, shown in Exhibit 3-6, to see details about the reminder or to dismiss the reminder. You can also set a snooze function to have the Reminders window open again, anywhere from 5 minutes to 2 weeks in the future.

Objective 1.3.3

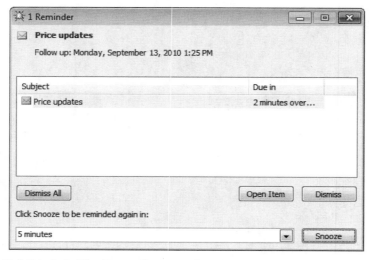

Exhibit 3-6: The Reminders window

Do it!

A-6: Using the Reminders window

Objective 1.3.3

Here's how	Here's why
1 Wait for the Reminders window to open	(If necessary.) You'll see the Price updates message that your partner sent to you.
2 Select the reminder and click **Open Item**	To open the message for which the reminder was set.
Close the message	
3 In the Reminders window, verify that the reminder item is selected, and click **Dismiss**	To remove the reminder.

Topic B: Managing junk e-mail

This topic covers the following Microsoft Office Specialist exam objectives for Outlook 2010.

#	Objective
3.3	**Manage junk mail**
	3.3.1 Allow a specific message (Not junk)
	3.3.2 Filter junk mail
	3.3.2.1 Never Block Sender
	3.3.2.2 Never Block Sender's Domain
	3.3.2.3 Never Block this Group or Mailing List
	3.3.2.4 Block Sender

Explanation

You might get unwanted or junk e-mail messages, which can clog your Inbox if they're not managed properly. *Junk e-mail messages* include unsolicited business promotion messages, advertisements, or messages with adult content. Outlook provides various tools to help you manage such messages. These tools include:

- The Junk E-Mail folder
- The Junk E-mail Filter
- The Blocked Senders list
- The Safe Senders list
- Additional options

The Junk E-Mail folder

Messages that Outlook determines to be junk are stored in a folder named Junk E-Mail. It is a good idea to review the messages in this folder from time to time to make sure they are not legitimate messages that you want to see.

Objective 3.3.1

If messages in your Junk E-Mail folder are legitimate, you can move them back to the Inbox. You can right-click the message and choose Junk, Not Junk, or you can simply drag the message to your Inbox (or any other folder). After you review the messages in your Junk E-Mail folder, you can empty the folder.

You can configure Outlook to automatically delete the messages it determines to be junk. If you do so, messages will not be moved to the Junk E-Mail folder. You will not have an opportunity to rescue misidentified, legitimate messages before they're deleted.

The Junk E-mail filter

Objective 3.3.2

Outlook examines the messages you receive to determine if they are legitimate or junk. It uses the rules defined in the Junk E-mail filter to make this determination. Your Exchange administrator can manage the rules associated with that filter. Users can set a sensitivity level:

- **No Automatic Filtering** — Junk e-mail filtering is disabled and all messages are delivered to your Inbox. You will have to manually manage junk e-mail if you use this option.
- **Low** — This default option is designed to catch the most obvious junk e-mail messages while catching the fewest legitimate messages.
- **High** — Most junk e-mail messages are caught, but a higher percentage of legitimate messages are misidentified as junk.
- **Safe Senders Lists Only** — Messages from anyone not on your Safe Senders or Safe Recipients lists will be marked as junk.

The Blocked Senders list

Objectives 3.3.2.1–3.3.2.4

You can block messages from a sender by adding the sender's e-mail address or domain name to the Blocked Senders list. When you do this, Outlook places any future messages from that sender in the Junk E-Mail folder. (In an Exchange environment, you cannot block senders within your own organization.)

There are at least three ways to add a sender to the Blocked Senders list:

- In the Folder Contents list, right-click a message from that sender and choose Junk, Block Sender.
- With a message from the sender open, click the Junk button in the Delete group on the Message tab and choose Block Sender.
- Click Junk and choose Junk E-mail Options to open the Junk E-mail Options dialog box. Click the Blocked Senders tab. Click Add, enter the offending address, and click OK.

The Safe Senders list

Objective 3.3.2.1

Messages from senders on your Safe Senders list are never treated as junk. In an Exchange environment, you cannot add senders in your own organization to your Safe Senders list, but they are treated as if they were on that list.

There are at least three ways to add a sender to the Safe Senders list:

- In the Folder Contents list, right-click a message from that sender and choose Junk, Never Block Sender.
- With a message from the sender open, click the Junk button in the Delete group on the Message tab and choose Never Block Sender.
- Click Junk and choose Junk E-mail Options to open the Junk E-mail Options dialog box. Click the Safe Senders tab. Click Add, enter the e-mail address, and click OK.

Additional options

Outlook includes additional features for managing junk e-mail. They are described in the following table.

Feature	Description
Safe Recipients list	E-mail sent to addresses on this list will never be treated as junk. Use this option to prevent mail addressed to e-mail lists and groups to which you belong from being treated as junk.
Postmarking	By default, Outlook stamps each outgoing message with a digital postmark. You could configure Outlook to treat messages that arrive without a postmark as junk. However, only Outlook supports this feature, so you would block potentially legitimate messages from senders using other e-mail applications.
Auto Picture Download	Senders of bulk junk e-mail use Web beacons to determine which addresses are legitimate and which are invalid. A *Web beacon* is a special type of image or file embedded in an e-mail message. When you view the image, a signal is sent to the sender, notifying him or her of your e-mail address. For this reason, by default, Outlook does not display pictures from Internet senders (those outside your organization).
International options	You can configure Outlook to automatically block mail from international domains. For example, many e-mail scams have originated in Nigeria. To block such messages, you could block all messages from the .ng domain. However, mailers of junk messages frequently falsify sender addresses, making domain-wide blocking a less than perfect way to filter junk e-mail.

Do it!

Objective 3.3

⚠ *If students click one of the blocking options, they will get a message stating that they can't block senders within their organization.*

B-1:   Exploring junk e-mail management features

Here's how	Here's why
1 Right-click a message from your partner	It does not matter which message.
Point to **Junk**	🔖 Block Sender Never Block Sender Never Block Sender's Domain (@example.com) Never Block this Group or Mailing List ✉ Not Junk Junk E-mail Options... To display the Junk E-mail menu. You could use the commands on this menu to add the sender to your Blocked Senders or Safe Senders lists.
2 Press (ESC) twice	To close the menus.

3 On the Home tab, in the Delete group, click **Junk**	To display the same menu.
Choose **Junk E-mail Options...**	To open the Junk E-mail Options dialog box.
4 Observe the four levels for handling junk e-mail	Choose the level of junk e-mail protection ○ <u>N</u>o Automatic Filtering. Mail from blocke Junk E-mail folder. ⦿ <u>L</u>ow: Move the most obvious junk e-ma ○ <u>H</u>igh: Most junk e-mail is caught, but sq as well. Check your Junk E-mail folder q ○ <u>S</u>afe Lists Only: Only mail from people q Senders List or Safe Recipients List will
	You could choose another protection level, but the default is suitable in most cases.
Observe the option to delete suspected junk e-mail	This setting deletes junk e-mail rather than storing it in your Junk E-Mail folder. You should probably not use this setting. Otherwise, you could miss legitimate e-mail that has been misidentified as junk.
5 Click the **Safe Senders** tab	Add senders to this list to be sure that mail from them is never considered to be junk.
6 Click the **Safe Recipients** tab	Add senders to this list so that mail addressed to them is not considered to be junk. Use this option for e-mail lists and groups you belong to.
7 Click the **Blocked Senders** tab	Add senders to this list to be sure that mail from them is always considered to be junk.
8 Click the **International** tab	Use the options here to manage the junk e-mail handling for messages from other countries.
9 Click **Cancel**	To close the dialog box without changing settings.

Topic C: Using Search folders

This topic covers the following Microsoft Office Specialist exam objectives for Outlook 2010.

#	Objective
1.4	Apply search and filter tools
	1.4.1 Use built-in Search folders

Explanation

Objective 1.4.1

In Outlook, you can use built-in Search folders to find messages in a specific category or based on a specific condition. For example, you could use a Search folder to find all messages containing specific text.

To add a Search folder:

1   In the Navigation Pane, click Mail.

2   In the Mail pane, right-click Search Folders and choose New Search Folder to open the New Search Folder dialog box, shown in Exhibit 3-7.

3   In the Select a Search Folder list, select a condition.

4   Click OK.

Exhibit 3-7: The New Search Folder dialog box

Do it!

Objective 1.4.1

TIPS

Tell students they can also press Ctrl+Shift+P.

Tell students that they might need to scroll down in the list box.

C-1: Setting up a Search folder

Here's how	Here's why
1 Activate the Mail pane	If necessary.
2 Right-click **Search Folders**	To display a shortcut menu.
Choose **New Search Folder...**	To open the New Search Folder dialog box.
3 Under Organizing Mail, select **Mail with specific words**	(In the Select a Search Folder list.) To specify the condition.
Click **Choose**	To open the Search Text dialog box.
4 In the box, type **Welcome**	As shown below.

Specify words or phrases to search for in the subject or body:

Welcome

Click **Add**	The word "Welcome" is added to the Search list.
Click **OK**	To close the Search Text dialog box.
5 Click **OK**	To close the New Search Folder dialog box and apply your search parameter.
6 Observe the Mail pane and the Folder Contents list	In the Mail pane, the Search Folders folder is expanded. Messages with the text "Welcome" in their subject or body appear in the Folder Contents list.
Click as shown	Search Folders Containing Welcome
	To collapse the Search Folders folder.

Using Search folders

Explanation

After creating a Search folder, you can use it to locate mail messages that satisfy the Search folder's condition. For example, you can create a Search folder to locate all messages to or from a specific client.

To see the messages in a Search folder, expand Search Folders in the Navigation pane and click the name of the Search folder you want to use. The folder's contents appear in the Folder Contents list.

Do it!

C-2: Using a Search folder

Objective 1.4.1

Here's how	Here's why
1 Open the Inbox folder	Activate the Mail pane and click Inbox.
2 Open a new Message window	
3 Address the message to your partner	
In the Subject box, enter **Welcome to the company**	
In the message area, enter **We're glad to have you on the Outlander Spices team!**	
4 Send the message	After a moment, your partner's e-mail message arrives in your Inbox.
5 Expand **Search Folders**	
6 Click **Containing Welcome (1)**	(This link is in the Mail pane.) To view the contents of the specific folder. The new message, with the word "Welcome" in the subject, appears in the Folder Contents list, along with all other messages containing "Welcome."
7 Open or preview the **Welcome to the company** message	To read the message.
Close the Message window	If necessary.
8 Click **Inbox**	To open your Inbox. The "Welcome to the company" message is in your Inbox. Search folders are "virtual" in that they help you find messages but don't actually contain messages.

Topic D: Printing messages and attachments

This topic covers the following Microsoft Office Specialist exam objectives for Outlook 2010.

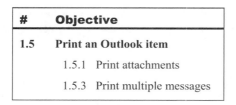

#	Objective
1.5	**Print an Outlook item**
	1.5.1 Print attachments
	1.5.3 Print multiple messages

Explanation

Objectives 1.5.1, 1.5.3

As with other Office documents, you can print Outlook messages. You can also control page settings such as margins, headers and footers, and orientation.

By using the options on the Print page, shown in Exhibit 3-8, you can specify which printer to use. You can also specify the style, the number of copies, and other settings for printouts. Click the File tab and choose Print to display these options.

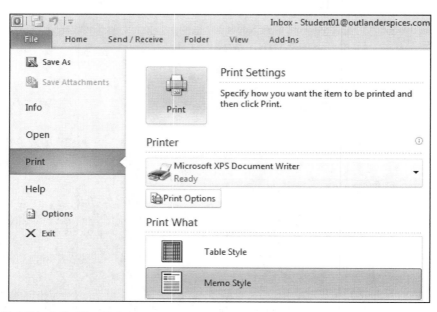

Exhibit 3-8: The Print page

The Print page displays a preview of the way your message will look when printed. From this page, you can specify which printer to print to. Use the Table Style option to print a list of messages in your Inbox (or currently selected folder). Use the Memo Style option to print the open or previewed e-mail message. Click the large Print button at the top of the page to actually print.

To customize the way messages print, you can change the page setup. The Page Setup: Memo Style dialog box is shown in Exhibit 3-9. You can use the Format, Paper, and Header/Footer tabs to specify the fonts, paper source, margins, orientation, and header and footer for the printed message. A header will appear at the top of the page, and the footer will appear at the bottom of the page. A page layout preview appears on the Format tab.

Tell students that their screens might look different.

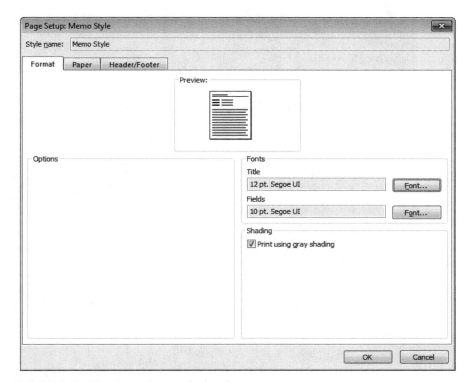

Exhibit 3-9: The Page Setup dialog box

To print a message, you can right-click it in the Inbox and choose Quick Print. The message will print to your default printer, and you won't be able to change any print settings. To print multiple messages, select each message you want to print; then click the File tab and click Print.

To print an attachment, you can double-click it to open it and then print it from within the application. Or you can right-click the attachment in an open message and choose Quick Print to print the attachment without changing any print settings.

Do it!

Objectives 1.5.1, 1.5.3

If you haven't given students access to a network printer, do that before you begin this activity.

D-1: Printing messages and attachments

Here's how	Here's why
1 Click **Inbox**	If necessary, to select your Inbox.
Select any message	In your Inbox.
2 Click the **File** tab and then click **Print**	To display the Print page. A large preview of your printout is shown on the right. In the middle are options for selecting the printer and the output style.
3 Click **Table Style**	The preview changes to show that a list of the messages in your Inbox will be printed instead of a single message.
4 Click **Print Options**	To open the Print dialog box. You can use controls in this dialog box to specify which printer to print to, how many copies to print, the range of pages to print, and so forth.
5 Select **Memo Style**	
Click **Page Setup**	To open the Page Setup dialog box.
6 Click the **Paper** tab	Use this tab to specify settings related to paper size and orientation.
7 Click **OK**	
8 Click **Print**	To print the message.
9 Return to the Inbox	
Select two messages	Use Ctrl+click to select them.
10 Click the **File** tab and click **Print**	
11 Preview the messages in the preview pane	
Click **Print**	To print both messages.
12 Open a message with an attachment	
Right-click the attachment and choose **Quick Print**	To print the attachment.

Unit summary: E-mail management

Topic A   In this topic, you learned how to set **importance** and **sensitivity levels** for messages. You also specified a **delayed delivery** for a message and specified an alternate address for e-mail replies. Then, you learned how to **flag messages** and mark flagged messages as completed. You also learned how to request a read receipt.

Topic B   In this topic, you learned how to manage **junk e-mail**. You learned how to add senders to the Blocked Senders list and add senders and domains to the Safe Senders List. Then you learned how to mark a message as Not Junk and empty the Junk E-Mail folder. You also learned how to change the **junk e-mail level** and configure other options for handling junk e-mail.

Topic C   In this topic, you learned how to create and use **Search folders**, which are used to find messages that meet a certain condition.

Topic D   In this topic, you learned how to customize the **page setup** when printing messages. You also learned how to **print** a message and an attachment.

Independent practice activity

In this activity, you'll specify a read receipt and an importance level for a new message. You'll flag a message, reply to a flagged message, and change your junk e-mail settings. You'll also add a sender to your Safe Senders list.

1 Compose a message with the text, **I forgot the date for the project-planning meeting. Can you please remind me?** Address the message to your partner.

2 Specify the subject as **Forgot**.

3 Set the options so that you receive a read receipt.

4 Set the importance level to High.

5 Send the message.

6 Read the message from your partner. When prompted, send a receipt.

7 Open the read receipt and read it. (*Hint:* Activate the Inbox.)

8 Close the Message window.

9 Create a flagged message to reply by 4:30 PM today, and send it to your partner. Enter any subject and message text. (*Hint:* In the Tags group on the Message tab, click Follow Up and choose Add Reminder. Check Flag for Recipients.)

10 Reply to the flagged message and mark it as completed.

11 Change the junk e-mail level to High. (*Hint:* Use the Junk E-mail Options dialog box.)

12 Add **samwilkens@doverspiceworks.com** to your Safe Senders list.

Review questions

1 On the Message tab, which group contains the buttons for setting the importance of a message?

A Send

B Tags

C Options

D Editing

2 What is the advantage of marking a message as private?

It prevents others from editing your original message when they reply to it or forward it.

3 What does a red exclamation mark indicate?

The message is marked as high importance.

4 How can you block messages from an entire domain?

Click Junk and choose Junk E-mail Options. On the Blocked Senders tab, click Add. Enter the e-mail address or domain name for the sender you want to block and click OK. Click OK to close the dialog box.

5 True or false? You should just delete all messages in your Junk E-Mail folder without reviewing them.

False. Sometimes legitimate e-mail messages will be sent to your Junk E-Mail folder. You should periodically review these messages.

6 What should you do if a legitimate message ends up in your Junk E-Mail folder?

Right-click the folder and choose Junk, Not Junk. The message will move to your Inbox.

7 When you're using a Search folder, when do you specify the condition that controls which messages are stored in the folder?

A After naming the folder

B After adding the folder to the Folder Contents list

C While creating the folder

D After saving the folder

8 What is the purpose of Search folders?

Search folders enable you to organize your mail messages by automatically displaying them in a folder based on specified criteria.

9 Name two ways to flag a message.

- *When creating a message, click Follow Up in the Options group and select a flag from the list.*

- *In the Folder Contents list, right-click the flag icon to display the flag options.*

10 When sending an urgent message, what can you do to be alerted when the recipient reads your message?

You can request a read receipt.

11 On which tab is the command to print an e-mail message?

The File tab.

Unit 4

Contacts

Unit time: 60 minutes

Complete this unit, and you'll know how to:

A Use the Contacts folder to add, modify, and organize business and personal contacts.

B Create and modify a contact group.

C Use the People Pane to view contact details.

Topic A: Working with contacts

This topic covers the following Microsoft Office Specialist exam objectives for Outlook 2010.

#	Objective
1.5	**Print an Outlook item**
	1.5.4 Print multiple contact records
2.5	**Attach content to e-mail messages**
	2.5.1 Attach an Outlook item
4.1	**Create and manipulate contacts**
	4.1.1 Modify a default business card
	4.1.2 Forward a contact
	4.1.3 Update a contact in the address book

Explanation

A *contact* is a person with whom you have either a business or personal relationship. You use the Contacts folder to manage information about each contact, such as the person's name, address, telephone number, e-mail address, Web site address, company name, birthday, and anniversary. The Contacts folder is integrated with the Inbox and the Calendar for sending e-mail and scheduling meetings. For example, when you enter a contact's birthday, it's automatically entered in the Calendar.

You can view the Contacts pane and folder by clicking Contacts in the Navigation pane. Outlook provides many methods of adding contacts to your address book.

Exhibit 4-1: A sample Contact window

Do it!

A-1: Exploring Contacts

Here's how	Here's why
1 In the Navigation pane, click **Contacts**	By default, the Contacts folder is empty.
2 Observe the Ribbon	Commands on the Home tab give you access to the most common functions you will use to manage your contacts.
3 Observe the buttons on the right side of the Folder Contents list	When you click any letter, the contact names beginning with the selected letter appear in the Folder Contents list, if the list is not empty.

Adding a contact

Explanation

⊒

Objective 4.1

There are various ways you can add a contact to your Contacts list. You can use the new Contact window, or add a contact from the header of a received e-mail message.

To add a contact by using the new Contact window:

1   Activate Contacts.

2   Click New Contact to open a new Contact window.

3   Enter information about the contact, such as the person's name, address, telephone number, and fax number.

4   In the Actions group, click Save & Close.

To add a contact from a received e-mail message:

1   Open or preview the message in the Reading pane.

2   In the message header, right-click the sender's e-mail address and choose Add to Outlook Contacts from the shortcut menu.

3   In the Contact window, enter any additional information needed.

4   Click Save & Close.

Do it!

Objective 4.1

A-2:   Adding contacts

Here's how	Here's why
1 Click **New Contact**	(In the New group on the Home tab for the Contacts pane.) To open a new Contact window.
2 In the Full Name box, enter **Richard Case**	To specify the name of the contact.
Press ⌶TAB⌷	To move the insertion point to the next box. The contact's name automatically appears in the format "last name, first name" in the File as list. This setting controls how Outlook saves contact information (alphabetically by last name).
3 In the Company box, enter **Western Spice Retailers**	To specify the contact's company name. This company is a customer of Outlander Spices.
Press ⌶TAB⌷	To move the insertion point to the next box.
4 In the Job title box, enter **Senior Buyer**	To specify the contact's job title.
5 In the E-mail address box, enter **fake@example.com**	
Press ⌶TAB⌷	Outlook creates the "Display as" text, using the contact's name and e-mail address.

6 Observe the text boxes under
   Phone numbers

There are four boxes for phone numbers:
Business, Home, Business Fax, and Mobile.

In the Business number box, enter
(585) 555-1212
and press ⟨TAB⟩

You can enter numbers in various formats,
including (585) 555-1212, 585.555.1212, and
585-555-1212.

If prompted, enter your area code
and click **OK** twice

To close the Location Information dialog box.

7 In the Addresses section, enter the
   address as shown

Outlook automatically checks "This is the
mailing address."

Depending on the size of the Contact window, students may need to click Show, and then select Details.

8 On the Contact tab, in the Show
   group, click **Details**

Here, you can enter details such as the contact's
manager, department, birthday, and anniversary.

In the Department box, enter
Marketing

On the Contact tab, click
General

To return to the general view.

9 In the Actions group, click
   Save & Close

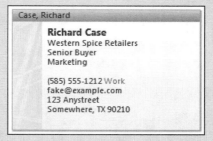

(On the Contact tab.) To save the contact
information and close the Contact window.

10 Display your Inbox

Click Mail in the Navigation pane.

11 Select a message from your
    partner

    In the Reading pane, right-click
    your partner's e-mail address

    Choose **Add to Outlook**
    Contacts

    To open a new Contact window, displaying your
    partner's contact information.

    If your partner is willing to share
    his or her full name, enter it in the
    Full Name box

    You can enter a fictitious name otherwise.

    Enter your partner's name in the
    Display as box

    Or use the fictitious name.

    Click **Save & Close**

If a Duplicate Contact
window appears, have
students click Update.

12 In the Reading pane, point to your
    partner's e-mail address

A pop-up is displayed, showing brief
information about the contact.

Modifying and saving contacts

Explanation

Objectives 4.1.1, 4.1.3

After creating a contact item, you might need to change the information. For example, if your client's address changes, you'll need to update the address accordingly. You can modify a contact and then save the changes as the current contact or as a new contact. You can also add various items—such as important documents, business cards, or messages—to your contacts.

To edit a contact, double-click it to open the Contact window. Then edit the information and save the contact. This saves the changes in the current contact file.

Do it!

A-3:   Modifying a contact

Objectives 4.1.1, 4.1.3

The files for this activity are in Student Data folder **Unit 4\Topic A**.

Here's how	Here's why
1 Activate Contacts	
2 Double-click **Richard Case**	To open a Contact window for Richard Case. You need to change the job title and add the e-mail address for this contact.
3 Edit the Job title box to read **Vice President**	
4 Click as shown	
5 Navigate to the current topic folder	Student Data folder Unit 4\Topic A.
Select **man1** and click **OK**	To add the picture to this contact.
6 Observe the business card preview	**Richard Case** Western Spice Retailers Vice President Marketing (585) 555-1212 Work fake@example.com 123 Anystreet Somewhere, TX 90210 The preview reflects your changes.
7 Click **Save & Close**	

Attaching items to contacts

Explanation

You can attach files and Outlook items to a contact. To attach a file, such as a Word document or Excel worksheet, open the contact. Click the Insert tab and click the Attach File button in the Include group. Select the file you want to attach and click Insert. The link to the file will appear in the Notes section. You can view the file by double-clicking its icon.

You can also attach Outlook items, such as a message, another contact, or an appointment, to a contact. Here's how:

1 Open the Contact.
2 Click the Insert tab and click the Attach Item button in the Include group.
3 From the Look in list, select the folder containing the item.
4 Select the desired item in the Items list and click Insert.

Do it!

A-4:   Attaching items to a contact

Here's how	Here's why
1 Open the **Richard Case** contact	(Double-click it.) You'll attach a Word document to the contact.
2 Click the **Insert** tab	
3 Click ![Attach File]	To open the Insert File dialog box.
Navigate to the current topic folder	
Select **Richard Case Bio**	
Click **Insert**	![Notes: Richard Case Bio.docx] An icon for the attached Word document appears in the Notes section.
4 Click the **Contact** tab	
Click **Save & Close**	

Adding contacts from the same company

Explanation

Several of your contacts might work for the same company. For these contacts, most of the information—such as the company name, the phone number, and the address—will be the same.

To save the time and effort spent in entering information for these contacts, you can select a contact from the same company, click New Items, and choose "Contact from Same Company." When you create a contact with this command, the company-related information appears automatically in the Contact window, as shown in Exhibit 4-2. You can then enter other details, such as the name and job title.

Exhibit 4-2: The new Contact window filled in with company information

A-5: Adding a contact from the same company

Here's how	Here's why
1 Verify that Richard Case is selected	In the Folder Contents list.
2 On the Home tab, in the New group, click **New Items** and choose **Contact from Same Company**	You'll add another contact from Western Spice Retailers. The name of the company, the business address, the business phone number, and the picture automatically appear in the Contact window, as shown in Exhibit 4-2.
3 In the Full Name box, enter **Michael Gos**	
In the Job title box, enter **Assistant Buyer**	
On the Contact tab, click **Picture** and choose **Remove Picture**	To remove the picture from this contact.
4 Save and close the contact information	Michael Gos appears as a contact in the Folder Contents list.

Forwarding and saving contacts

Explanation

Objectives 2.5.1, 4.1.2

If a colleague needs the information for one of your contacts, instead of typing a contact's information into a message, simply attach the contact to an e-mail message. Create a message and click Attach Item. From the Look in list, select Contacts. Under Items, select the contact you want to attach, and then click OK.

You can also save a contact attachment as a contact record. To do so:

1   Open the e-mail message.

2   Double-click the contact attachment. The Contact window containing the contact's information will appear.

3   Click Save & Close to save the contact in your Contacts.

A-6: Forwarding and saving contacts

The files for this activity are in Student Data folder **Unit 4\Topic A**.

Here's how	Here's why
1 Create another contact, from Western Spice Retailers, named **Jill Smith##**	Where ## is your number.
Set the picture to one of the sample female photos	Click Picture and choose Change Picture. Navigate to the current topic's data folder. Select a photo and click Open.
2 Save and close the contact	
3 Click **Mail**	(In the Navigation pane.) You'll send the Jill Smith contact to your partner.
4 Create a message, addressed to your partner, with the subject **Jill Smith**	
5 Click **Attach Item**	(In the Include group.) You'll attach the Jill Smith contact to the message.
Choose **Business Card**, **Other Business Cards...**	In Outlook terminology, a contact you send is called a business card.
Select **Smith##, Jill**	
Click **OK**	
6 Send the message	
7 Select the **Jill Smith** message	This is the message from your partner. You can see the contact card in the preview window
8 Double-click where indicated	

o: Student01

✉ Message   📇 Jill Smith02.vcf (9 KB)

	The Contact window appears.
Click **Save & Close**	To save the contact and close the window.
9 Close the message window	If you opened the message rather than previewing it.
10 Click **Contacts**	(In the Navigation pane.) Your partner's Jill Smith## contact is listed with the rest of your contacts.

Using Contacts folder views

Explanation

Outlook offers several views for each folder. A *view* is the way the data appears in the Folder Contents list. In Contacts, the default view is Business Cards. In this view, you can see the person's name, company information, phone numbers, fax number, e-mail address, and company address for each contact.

To change the view for the Contacts folder, select the view you want to use from the Current View list in the Contacts pane.

Do it!

A-7: Viewing your contacts

Here's how	Here's why
1 Observe the Folder Contents list	Each contact appears as a business address card. These cards are sorted alphabetically and show a few important details, such as a contact's address and phone numbers.
2 On the Home tab, in the Current View group, click **Card**	Case, Richard Full Name: Rich... Job Title: Vice... Company: Wes... Department: Mar... Business: 123 Ar Som... Business: (585... E-mail: fake... To display the contact information by company name.
3 Click **Phone**	To display an alphabetized list of all your contacts.
4 To the right of Phone, click ▾	To display more view options.
5 Select **List**	To display a list categorized by company and then sorted alphabetically.
6 Select the **Business Card** view	Click the up arrow and then click Business Card.

Depending on the width of students' screens, they might have to click the arrow button shown in Step 4.

Customizing electronic business cards

Explanation

Objective 4.1.1

You can control what information an electronic business card contains. To do so, open the contact and click Business Card in the Options group on the Contact tab. This opens the Edit Business Card dialog box, shown in Exhibit 4-3. Here, you can change which content will be displayed by changing the fields that appear on the business card. These fields correspond to the fields in the Contact window.

You can change which fields are displayed on your card by adding or removing them in the Fields list:

- To add a field to the list and display its content on the card, click Add and select a field from the list.
- To prevent a field from being included on the card, select its field name under Fields and click Remove. If you want to add a field back, all you need to do is click Add and select it from the list.

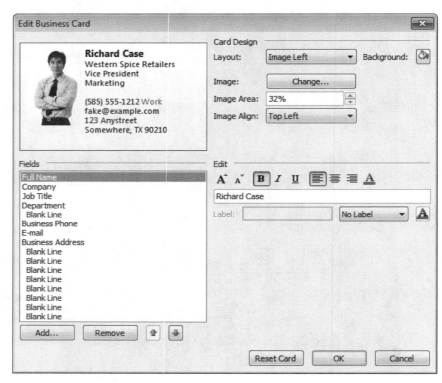

Exhibit 4-3: The Edit Business Card dialog box

Moving fields

With an electronic business card, you're not stuck with any particular order of content display. You can move the fields around. To move a field up or down on the electronic business card, select the field in the list and then click the arrow buttons at the bottom of the dialog box.

Editing field values

You can edit the values of fields in the Edit Business Card dialog box. To do so, select a field and edit the value under Edit. Keep in mind that when you edit the value of a field for the business card, you are also editing it for the associated contact.

If you delete a field value, it will be removed from the electronic business card and from the contact. If you don't want a field displayed on the card, use the Remove button instead.

Do it!

Objective 4.1.1

A-8:   Editing an electronic business card

Here's how	Here's why
1 Open the **Richard Case** contact	
2 On the Contact tab, in the Options group, click **Business Card**	To edit the contact's business card.
3 In the list of fields, select **Department**	To display a menu. You'll remove the Department field from the business card.
Click **Remove**	
4 In the list of fields, after Business Address, select **Blank Line**	You're selecting the first "Blank Line" item following Business Address.
Click ⬆	Fields Full Name Company Job Title Blank Line Business Phone E-mail Blank Line Business Address To add a blank line before the business address.
5 In the list of fields, select **Business Phone**	You'll edit the label that identifies this field.
6 In the Label box, enter **(W)**	
Under Edit, click **B**	To make the phone number and its label bold.
From the Label position list, select **Left**	
7 Observe the card preview	**Richard Case** Western Spice Retailers Vice President (w) **(585) 555-1212** fake@example.com 123 Anystreet Somewhere, TX 90210
8 Click **OK**	To save your changes and return to the Contact editing window.
9 Click **Save & Close**	This contact's card reflects your changes. The other cards use the default layout.

Printing contacts

Explanation

Objective 1.5.4

You can print contacts by using the settings accessible from the File tab, or you can select a single contact, right-click it, and choose Quick Print. If you use the File tab, you can choose from the following styles:

- **Card Style** — The contacts appear as business cards.
- **Small Booklet Style** — The information for multiple contacts is printed, using a small font.
- **Medium Booklet Style** — The information for multiple contacts is printed, using a larger font than the one used with the Small Booklet Style.
- **Memo Style** — Each full contact is printed on a separate page.
- **Phone Directory Style** — Contacts are printed alphabetically by name, with only phone numbers included.

Do it!

Objective 1.5.4

A-9: Printing contacts

Here's how	Here's why
1 Right-click a contact and choose **Quick Print**	To print a single contact in Memo Style.
2 Click the **File** tab and then click **Print**	To display the Print page.
3 Observe the different styles	You have several options for printing single contacts or multiple contacts.
4 Select **Small Booklet Style**	
Click **Print**	To print your contacts.
5 Close any open windows	

Topic B: Using contact groups

This topic covers the following Microsoft Office Specialist exam objectives for Outlook 2010.

#	Objective
2.1	**Create and send e-mail messages**
	2.1.10 Send a message to a contact group
4.2	**Create and manipulate contact groups**
	4.2.1 Create a contact group
	4.2.2 Manage contact group membership

Explanation

Contact groups simplify the steps you must take to e-mail a group of people. Normally, you would need to add each recipient to the To box of your message. Instead, you can address the message to your contact group, and Outlook will send copies to every member of the group.

A *contact group*, formerly known as a distribution list, is a collection of e-mail addresses. You assign a name to a contact group. To send e-mail to members of the group, address your message to the group's name.

Creating contact groups

Objective 4.2.1

Your Exchange administrator can create contact groups in the Global Address List. You can create them in your personal Contacts folder.

To create a contact group in your Contacts folder:

1   On the Home tab, in the New group, click New Contact Group to open a new Contact Group window, as shown in Exhibit 4-4.
2   In the Name box, enter the name you want to use for the group.
3   In the Members group on the Contact Group tab, click Add Members. Then choose one of these three options:
   - **From Outlook Contacts** — Displays names from your local Contacts list.
   - **From Address Book** — Displays names from the global Exchange address book.
   - **New E-mail Contact** — Enables you to enter an e-mail address directly.
4   Select a member from the Name list and click Members.
5   Repeat step 4 until all the desired members are selected. Then click OK.
6   In the Actions group, click Save & Close.

If you have multiple members to add, you can select them in step 4 by pressing Ctrl, clicking each member you want to include, and clicking Members. You also can enter e-mail addresses by typing them in the Members box at the bottom of the dialog box. Enter a semicolon (;) after each member you add manually.

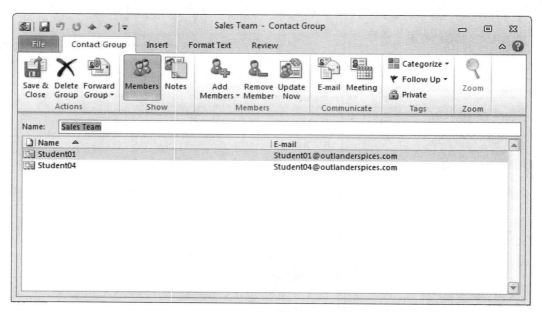

Exhibit 4-4: The Sales Team - Contact Group window

Using contact groups

Objective 2.1.10

One way to send a message to a contact group is to right-click the group and choose Create, E-Mail. This opens a new Message window. In the To box, the name of the contact group is underlined, indicating that the group is valid. You can then compose and send the message, which will be delivered to everyone in the group.

Another way to send a message to a contact group is to create an e-mail message and enter the name of the contact group in the To box. As you type the first few letters of the group's name, the rest of the name will appear, and you can press Enter to enter it.

Do it!

Objectives 2.1.10, 4.2.1

TIPS *Students can also press Ctrl+Shift+L.*

B-1: Creating and using a contact group

Here's how	Here's why
1 Click **Contacts**	(If necessary.) In the Navigation pane.
2 On the Home tab, click **New Contact Group**	In the New group.
3 In the Name box, enter **Sales Team**	This will be the name of your contact group.
4 In the Members group, click **Add Members** and choose **From Address Book**	To open the Select Members dialog box. You'll add members to the Sales Team group.
From the Name list, select **Student01**	
Click **Members**	To add Student01 to your contact group.
5 Add Student04	Select Student04 and click Members.
Click **OK**	To close the Select Members dialog box. The Contact Group window appears, as shown in Exhibit 4-4.
6 Click **Save & Close**	Sales Team / **Sales Team** / Group To save the Sales Team contact group. It now appears as a contact in the Folder Contents list.
7 Right-click **Sales Team**	
Choose **Create**, **E-mail**	To... ⊞ **Sales Team** To open a new Message window. Sales Team appears in the To box. The name has been automatically checked and validated against the Global Address List.
8 Send the message with the subject **Distribution Sales Report**	

Tell students that if they click the plus sign, all members of the list will appear. After the list is expanded, it can't be collapsed.

Tell students that only Student01 and Student04 will receive the messages.

Modifying contact groups

Explanation

Objective 4.2.2

After you've created a contact group, you might need to add or remove members. You also might need to change a member's information, such as by adding a new e-mail address or phone number.

To add a new member to the contact group:

1 Open the contact group.
2 On the Contact Group tab, in the Members group, click Add Members and choose the appropriate source.
3 Select or add the contact.
4 Click Save & Close.

If you want to add a member who is already in your address book, then open the contact group, click Add Members, and choose From Address Book. Select the member you want to add, click Members, and click OK.

To remove a member from the contact group, open the group. Select the member you want to remove and click Remove Member in the Members group.

Updating contact details

Contact details change. If you update an entry in your contacts, that information will not be automatically reflected in your contact group. You should make sure to update your contact group after modifying contact details. To do so:

1 Open the contact group.
2 On the Contact Group tab, in the Members group, click Update Now.

When editing your contact group, you can update a member's details with a simple double-click as long as he or she is not in your organization. Otherwise, you must add her or him to your contacts list first and then update the information.

To update a member's information:

1 Open the contact group.
2 Double-click the member's name.

   If he or she is not in your organization, this will open the Contact window, where you can edit this person's details.

   If the member is part of your organization, double-clicking the entry will display the contact card. As shown in Exhibit 4-5, display the View more options menu and choose Add to Outlook Contacts. (Use this same command to edit a contact that is already in your Contacts list.)

3 Enter the new information. Click Save & Close to return to the Contact Group window.
4 Click Save & Close.

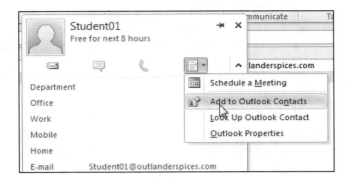

Exhibit 4-5: Adding a group member to your Contacts

To send the updated information to the entire contact group:

1   Create an e-mail message, click To, locate and double-click the contact group, and click OK.

2   In the Include group, click Attach Item.

3   From the Look in list, select Contacts.

4   From the Items list, select the contact group. Click OK.

5   Complete and send the message.

B-2: Modifying a contact group

Here's how	Here's why
1 Activate Contacts	(If necessary.) You'll add and remove members of the Sales Team contact group.
2 Double-click the **Sales Team** contact group	To open the Sales Team Contact Group window.
3 Click **Add Members** and choose **From Outlook Contacts**	
Select **Richard Case**	
Click **Members** and click **OK**	
4 Double-click **Richard Case**	In the list of members. He is not in your organization, so the Contact window opens.
Edit the e-mail address to be **rcase@westernspices.com**	
Click **Save & Close**	To save the new information.
5 Double-click **Student01**	This member is part of your organization, so the contact card is displayed.
Click ▤ ▾	The View more options button.
Choose **Add to Outlook Contacts**	After adding this member to your Contacts, you can edit his or her details.
In the Company box, enter **Outlander Spices**	
Click **Save & Close**	To save the contact in your Contacts list.
6 Double-click **Student01**	
Click ▤ ▾	Even though you already added the contact, you would still use the Add to Outlook Contacts command to edit this person's details.
Press (ESC) twice	To close the menu and the contact card.
7 Select **Student04**	You'll remove this member from the contact group.
Click **Remove Member**	In the Members group on the Ribbon.
8 Click **Save & Close**	Student01 is listed with your other contacts.

Topic C: Using the People Pane

This topic covers the following Microsoft Office Specialist exam objectives for Outlook 2010.

#	Objective
1.3	**Arrange the Content pane**
	1.3.4 Use the People Pane

Explanation

A new feature of Outlook 2010 is the *Outlook Social Connector* (OSC). This system is meant to interconnect Outlook with various social networks. For example, with appropriate components installed, you could see a contact's LinkedIn status updates within Outlook.

Objective 1.3.4

Support for OSC is built into Outlook. However, third-party software developers must provide the actual software to connect Outlook to a social network. For example, LinkedIn connectivity is provided by a component published by the LinkedIn Corporation. Microsoft provides a connector for SharePoint services.

Even without adding an OSC component, you can use the new People Pane (which is where those social network updates would be displayed). Without a connector, the People Pane will still display information about your contacts, including their names and pictures. With a simple click, you can view calendar information, contact details, and more.

Exhibit 4-6: The People Pane at the bottom of a message

The People Pane, shown in Exhibit 4-6, is displayed at the bottom of the Reading pane, as well as at the bottom of the Message window when you read or compose an e-mail message. An icon is shown for each person on the To, From, CC, and BCC lines. By default, the sender's icon is left-aligned within the pane. On the right are icons for everyone who was party to the message (including the sender).

Do it!

Objective 1.3.4

C-1: Examining the People Pane

Here's how	Here's why
1 Activate Mail	View your Inbox.
2 Select the **Welcome to Outlook 2010** message	You might need to scroll down.
3 Observe the People Pane	(At the bottom of the Reading pane.) It shows generic icons for each recipient, plus the Instructor.
4 Point to the rightmost icon in the People Pane	A tooltip displays the contact's name and the source of the address: Contacts or Global Address List.
5 Create an e-mail message	
6 Add your partner to the To line	After you press Tab or Enter, an icon for his or her contact record is displayed in the People Pane.
7 Close the message without sending it	Click the Close button, and then click No so you don't save a copy of the message.

People Pane icons

Explanation

Objective 1.3.4

By default, generic icons are shown for each contact in the People Pane. If you have assigned a picture to a contact, that photo will be used instead of the icon. According to Microsoft's documentation, if you connect to a social network, the user's icon (or avatar) on that network will be used in your People Pane.

You can expand the People Pane to show additional details for each contact. If you have connected to a social network, you will see a person's status updates in the expanded view. Without a connector, you will be able to view recent e-mail messages, attachments, and calendar details. Exhibit 4-7 shows the expanded People Pane.

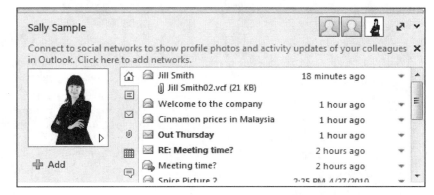

Exhibit 4-7: The expanded People Pane shows additional details

Do it!

Objective 1.3.4

C-2: Viewing custom photos in the People Pane

The files for this activity are in Student Data folder **Unit 4\Topic C**.

Here's how	Here's why
1 In the Navigation pane, click **Contacts**	
2 Double-click your partner's card	To open it for editing.
3 Click the picture placeholder as shown	
4 Navigate to the current topic folder	This folder contains sample photos that you can use to represent your partner.
5 Select a photo	There are various photos for you to choose from, though none will be a photo of your partner.
Click **Open**	To assign the picture to your contact entry for your partner's e-mail address.
6 Make sure you have entered your partner's name in both the Full Name and Display As boxes	You can use a fictitious name, such as Sally Sample, if your partner doesn't want to share his or her full name with you.
7 Click **Save & Close**	
8 In the Navigation pane, click **Mail**	To view your Inbox
9 Select the **Welcome to Outlook 2010** message	(If necessary.) The People Pane now shows the photo you selected instead of the generic icon.
10 In the People Pane, click your partner's icon	
	The People Pane expands to show additional details, including recent communications you've had with your partner.
Click ⌄	To collapse the People Pane to a single line again.

Contact details

Explanation

Objective 1.3.4

In a message or preview window, you can view details of the contact associated with the message by pointing to the person's name. When you point to the name, a pop-up that Microsoft also calls the People Pane is displayed. Because it looks vaguely like an old-fashioned Rolodex® card, we'll call it a "contact card" to distinguish it from the bar at the bottom of the Reading and Message panes.

Exhibit 4-8: The "contact card" shows details for a contact

The contact card shows the contact's photo and name. Additionally, if you're connected via an Exchange server, the card will inform you of the contact's upcoming availability. Below the contact's photo and name are buttons you can use to work with this person:

- Click the first button on the left to compose an e-mail message to this contact.
- The next two icons can be used to send an instant message or make a phone call to the contact. Both options require you to sign onto an instant messaging service or similar digital messaging system enabled by your administrator.
- Click the fourth button to display additional options, such as scheduling a meeting with the contact, adding him or her to your Contacts list, and so forth.
- Click the down-arrow button to display additional details for the contact.

Pinning a contact card

Normally, if you click elsewhere within the Outlook window, the contact card will close. However, you can click the pushpin button to "pin" the window, which means that it will stay open until you click the pushpin again or click the Close button. You can even drag the contact card outside of the Outlook window, as shown in Exhibit 4-9; this feature might be useful on a large monitor or with a dual-monitor workstation.

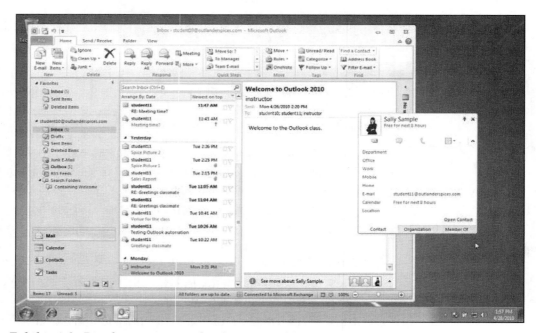

Exhibit 4-9: Pin the contact card to keep it visible

Do it!

Objective 1.3.4

C-3: Viewing contact details

The files for this activity are in Student Data folder **Unit 4\Topic C**.

Here's how	Here's why
1 Select the **Welcome to Outlook 2010** message	If necessary.
2 In the message header in the preview, point to your account name	The contact card is displayed.
3 In the message header in the preview, point to your partner's name	The contact card is displayed. If the photo you selected for your partner is not showing, keep pointing to your partner's name; the photo will appear after a few moments.
4 Click [icon]	To open a new Message window. Your partner's e-mail address is automatically entered into the To box.
Close the Message window	Without sending or saving the message.
5 In the message header in the preview, point to your partner's name	To display the contact card again.
6 Click [pin icon]	To pin the card open.
7 Click [icon]	To open a new Message window. The contact card stays open, even though it is behind the Message window.
8 Close the Message window	Without sending or saving the message.
9 Click [X]	To close the contact card.

Unit summary: Contacts

Topic A   In this topic, you used the Contacts folder to **create** and **edit contacts**. You also added contacts from the same company. Then you used different **views** of your Contacts folder. Finally, you edited and formatted a contact's **electronic business card**.

Topic B   In this topic, you created and used **contact groups**, which make it easier to send a message to multiple recipients. You also added and removed members of a contact group and updated member information.

Topic C   In this topic, you explored the **People Pane**. You set a custom picture for a contact and viewed it in the People Pane. You also viewed the "contact card" and used its buttons to compose a message and **pin** the card open.

Independent practice activity

In this activity, you'll add contacts, create a contact group, and address a new message to a specified contact group.

1 Add Peter Greenfield's contact information as shown in Exhibit 4-10. Save the contact information.

2 Add **Scott Bates** as a new contact from the same company as Peter Greenfield, and specify his job title as **Marketing Director**. Save the contact information.

3 Create a contact group with the name **Purchase Team**. Add Student03 and Student04 as members. Save the information.

4 Send a message to Purchase Team with the subject **Requirements** and a brief message of your choice.

5 Add the e-mail address **pgreenfield@wonderlandhotels.com** to the Peter Greenfield contact.

6 On Peter Greenfield's electronic business card, change the label for the phone number to **Phone:** and move it to the left side.

7 Remove +1 from the phone number value.

8 Save and close the business card.

9 Save and close the contact.

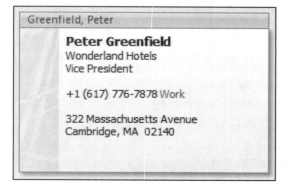

Exhibit 4-10: The contact information to be added in Step 1

Review questions

1 What steps do you follow to create a contact?

 a *Activate Contacts.*

 b *Click New Contact to open a new Contact window.*

 c *Enter the contact information.*

 d *Click Save & Close.*

2 How do you edit a contact?

 Double-click the contact in the Folder Contents list, make the necessary edits, and click Save & Close.

3 Name the four views available in the Contacts folder.

 Business Card, Card, Phone, and List.

4 How do you create a contact from a received e-mail message?

 Open or preview the message. Right-click the sender's e-mail address and choose Add to Outlook Contacts. Fill in any additional information and click Save & Close.

5 How do you create a new contact that works for the same company as one of your previous contacts?

 Select the contact that belongs to that company. On the Home tab, click New Items and choose Contact from Same Company. Make the necessary edits and click Save & Close.

6 What is the advantage of creating a contact group?

 A contact group enables you to send the same message to multiple recipients as a single entry.

7 How do you send a message to a contact group?

 You can do either of the following:

 • *Create a message, and enter the name of the contact group in the To box.*

 • *Select the contact group, and click E-mail in the Communicate group on the Home tab.*

8 How do you create an electronic business card?

 Simply create a new contact.

9 Can you modify the information shown in an electronic business card?

 Yes. Open the contact and click Business Card. In the Edit Business Card dialog box, you can add, remove, and reposition fields.

10 How do you send an electronic business card to another person?

 Create a message. In the Include group, click Attach Item and choose Business Card. If you've previously sent the card, it will be listed on the menu. Otherwise, choose Other Business Cards, select the card you want to send, and click OK. Finish composing your message and click Send.

11 Where is the People Pane visible?

 It is shown at the bottom of the Reading pane when you are previewing a message. It also appears at the bottom of the Message window when you are reading or composing a message.

Unit 5

Tasks

Unit time: 40 minutes

Complete this unit, and you'll know how to:

A Use the Tasks folder and the To-Do Bar to create, edit, and delete single and recurring tasks; insert a task into a message; and categorize and view your tasks.

B Use the Tasks folder to assign tasks, accept or decline a task request, send a status report, and track the completion of an assigned task.

Topic A: Working with tasks

This topic covers the following Microsoft Office Specialist exam objectives for Office 2010.

#	Objective
6.1	**Create and manipulate tasks**
	6.1.1 Create a task
	6.1.2 Manage task details
	6.1.4 Mark a task as complete
	6.1.9 Use Current View

Explanation

In Outlook, a *task* is an activity that must be completed within a specified period of time. A task has a current *status*, which can be In Progress, Not Started, Waiting on someone else, Deferred, or Completed. You can assign a Low, Normal, or High priority to a task, and you can track its completion by setting a percent-complete value.

You can create tasks and monitor their status in the *To-Do Bar's Task list* or in the *Tasks folder*. After creating a task, you can edit or delete it. In addition, you can send a task through e-mail as an attachment.

The To-Do Bar's Task list and the Tasks folder store the tasks you need to perform—both those you created and those that another person has assigned to you. To display the Tasks folder, click Tasks in the Navigation pane.

Exhibit 5-1 shows the Outlook window with the Tasks pane active. The list of tasks appears in the Folder Contents list, and the same list appears in the Task list in the To-Do Bar.

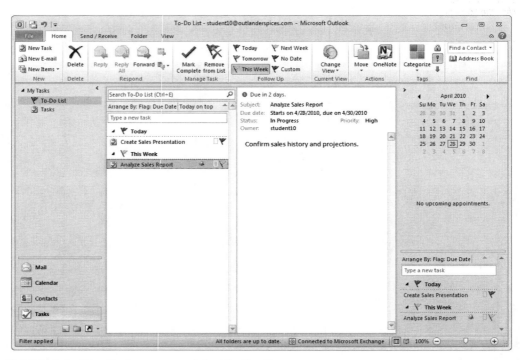

Exhibit 5-1: The Tasks pane and the To-Do Bar

Do it!

A-1: Exploring the Tasks folder and the To-Do Bar

Here's how	Here's why

1 In the Navigation pane, click **Tasks**

2 Observe the Folder pane

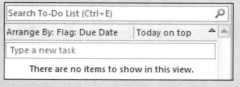

You have no tasks defined. Using the boxes in the Folder pane, you can search for, change your view of, and create tasks.

Tell students to click the sideways-caret button to expand the To-Do Bar if it is hidden.

3 Observe the To-Do Bar

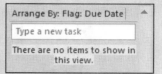

The "Type a new task" box and the Task list are located at the bottom of the To-Do Bar.

4 Observe the Home tab

Task-specific buttons are now available.

Objective 6.1.9

If students' screens are wide enough, the Current View group will list three views. To see the list shown here, students can click the More button, which is the down-pointing double triangle.

5 In the Current View group, click **Change View**

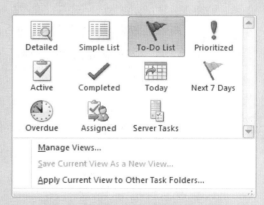

(Or click the More button.) To display a list of view options. To-Do List is the default view.

Press (ESC)

Creating and deleting tasks

Explanation

Objective 6.1.1

There are several ways you can create a task:

- With the Tasks pane active, click New Task on the Home tab. With this method, you will open a Task window, as shown in Exhibit 5-2.
- With the Tasks pane active, enter a task title in the "Type a new task" box in the Folder pane. The Task window is not displayed; double-click your task to open it.
- Enter a task title in the "Type a new task box" in the To-Do Bar. The Task window is not displayed; double-click your task to open it.
- Flag an e-mail message to add it to your To-Do Bar's Task list. The Task window is not displayed; double-click your task to open it.

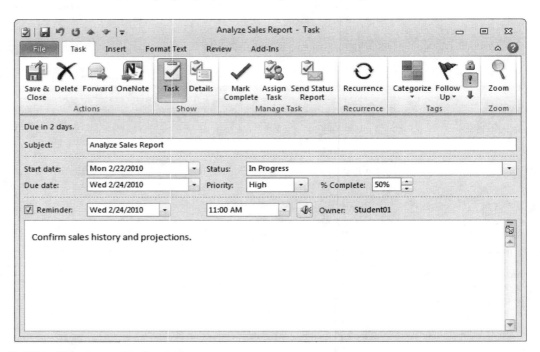

Exhibit 5-2: A new Task window

When creating or editing a task, you can enter details, such as a Start date, Due date, Status, Priority, % Complete, and Reminder. (See Exhibit 5-2 for examples.) After entering your task details, click Save & Close.

You can quickly create tasks by using the "Type a new task" box in the Folder pane or the To-Do Bar. When you do so, the task will be assigned today's date for the due date and start date. The priority will be set to Normal, and the status will be set to Not Started. Double-click the task to edit it.

The Task window

In the new Task window, the Show group on the Task tab contains two buttons: Task and Details. Click the Task button if you want to enter such information as the subject, start and end dates, status, and priority. Click the Details button if you want to enter such information as the total work estimated, the actual time taken, and expenses incurred to complete the task.

Deleting a task

Deleting a task removes it from your Tasks folder. Deleting a task is different from marking it as completed. When you mark a task as completed, Outlook retains a record of the work you've done. When you delete a task, it is moved to your Deleted Items folder.

To delete a task, do any of the following:

- Select the task and then click Delete on the Home tab.
- Right-click the task and choose Delete.
- Double-click the task to open the Task window. Click Delete on the Task tab.

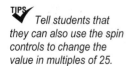

Do it!

Objective 6.1.1

A-2:   **Creating and deleting tasks**

Here's how	Here's why
1 On the Home tab, click **New Task**	To open a new Task window. You'll create a task for analyzing a sales report. The report has to be analyzed and the feedback has to be sent within two days.
2 In the Subject box, enter **Analyze Sales Report**	To specify the subject of the task.
3 Observe the Start and Due dates	They are blank by default.
4 Click the arrow next to the Start date box	To display the Date Navigator.
Select today's date	You'll start this task today.
5 Set the Due date to two days after of the current date	ⓘ Due in 2 days. Subject: Analyze Sales Report To specify the due date. The InfoBar indicates that the task is due in two days.
6 From the Status list, select **In Progress**	To specify that this task is in progress.
7 From the Priority list, select **High**	To specify the importance of the task.
8 Edit the % Complete box to read **50%**	To specify the percentage of the task that is completed.
9 Check **Reminder**	To set a reminder for the task. By default, you will be reminded on the due date. You could set another date.
10 From the Reminder time list, select **11:00 AM**	To specify the time when the reminder should appear.

TIPS *Tell students that they can also use the spin controls to change the value in multiples of 25.*

11 In the description box, enter **Confirm sales history and projections.**	To enter a description of what this task entails.
12 Click **Save & Close**	The task appears in the Folder Contents list, and a preview of it appears in the Preview pane.
13 In the Folder pane, in the "Type a new task" box, type **Create Sales Presentation** Press ⟵ ENTER	

	Your task is created, with its due date set to Today.
14 Create a task named **Lunch with Bob**	Enter it in the "Type a new task" box.
15 In the Folder Contents list, select **Lunch with Bob** Click **Delete**	You'll delete this task because it would be more appropriate to create this type of item as a Calendar entry rather than as a task. (On the Home tab.) To delete the task.

Editing tasks

Explanation

Objective 6.1.2

As you work on your tasks, the status or the percentage completed will change. To reflect these changes, you'll need to edit the task information. You can edit such information as the status, the due date, and the percentage of completion. You can also mark tasks as private.

To edit a task:

1 Open the task.

2 Change the due date, status, priority, and percent complete, as needed.

3 Click Save & Close.

Do it!

Objective 6.1.2

Tell students they can also double-click the task in the To-Do Bar's Task list.

A-3: Editing a task

Here's how	Here's why
1 In the Folder Contents list, double-click **Create Sales Presentation**	You'll edit this task.
2 Set the start date to be three days from now	
3 Set the due date to be four days from now	
4 From the Status list, select **Deferred**	To specify that the task has been delayed or postponed.
5 Save and close the task	The task changes are reflected in the Folder Contents list.

Setting up recurring tasks

Explanation

A *recurring task* is a task that needs to be performed on a regular basis. To create a recurring task, you need to specify the pattern in which the task recurs. For example, you can create a task for the first Monday of every month or the fourth Wednesday of every April. This is called the *recurrence pattern*, which can be annual, monthly, weekly, or daily. You also need to specify the *range of recurrence*, which indicates the starting and ending dates for the recurring task, as shown in Exhibit 5-3.

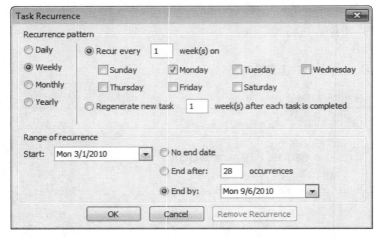

Exhibit 5-3: Scheduling a recurring task

To create a recurring task:

Objective 6.1.1

1   Open a new Task window.

2   Enter the necessary information.

3   On the Task tab, in the Recurrence group, click Recurrence to open the Task Recurrence dialog box.

4   Specify settings for the recurrence pattern and click OK.

5   Click Save & Close.

Do it!

Objective 6.1.1

A-4:   Adding a recurring task

Here's how	Here's why
1 Create a task with the subject **Generate Sales Report**	Open a new Task window, and enter the subject "Generate Sales Report."
	You need to send a sales report to a manager every Monday for the next six months. Instead of creating a task every week, you'll create a recurring task.
Specify the start date as next Monday	Click the arrow next to the Start date box to display the Date Navigator, and select the next Monday.
2 On the Task tab, click **Recurrence**	(In the Recurrence group.) To open the Task Recurrence dialog box.
3 Under Recurrence pattern, select **Weekly**	(If necessary.) To specify that this task has to be performed every week.
Select **Recur every**	If necessary.
Enter **1**	If necessary.
Check **Monday**	If necessary.
4 Examine the options under "Range of recurrence"	You can specify the start and end dates of the recurrence period. You specify the start date in the Start box. By default, no end date is selected. If you know the number of occurrences, use the "End after" option to specify that number. If the recurring task ends on a specific date, use the "End by" option.
Select **End by**	
Display the Date Navigator and select the Monday six months from the start date	Click the arrow next to the End by box to display the Date Navigator.
5 Click **OK**	
6 Save the task	

Help students find the Recurrence button.

① Due in 5 days.
    Starts every Monday effective 5/3/2010 until 11/1/2010.

Subject: Generate Sales Report

To close the Task Recurrence dialog box and save the settings. The InfoBar summarizes the details of the recurring task.

▲ ▼ **Next Week**

      Generate Sales Report

The task is marked with a recurring-task icon in the Folder Contents list.

TIPS *Tell students that if the task is overdue, the task details will appear in red in the Folder Contents list.*

Marking tasks as completed

Explanation

Objective 6.1.4

When you complete a task, you change its status to Complete. Outlook then marks the task as completed. There are several ways to mark a task as completed:

- In the Folder Contents list, select the task and click Mark Complete on the Home tab.
- In the Folder Contents list or the To-Do Bar's Task list, right-click the task and choose Mark Complete from the shortcut menu.
- Open the task and enter "100%" in the % Complete box.
- Open the task and select Completed from the Status list.
- In Tasks view, check the checkbox next to the task name.

Completed tasks are not shown in the To-Do list or the To-Do Bar. In Tasks view, completed tasks are formatted with a strikethrough line across their names.

Do it!

Objective 6.1.4

A-5: Marking a task as completed

Here's how	Here's why
1 Select the **Analyze Sales Report** task	
2 Click **Mark Complete**	(On the Home tab.) The task is removed from the Folder pane.
3 In the Navigation pane, beneath My Tasks, click **Tasks**	▲ My Tasks ‹ ⌇ To-Do List ⌇ Tasks To change to Tasks view. The completed task is shown in this view.
4 Double-click the **Analyze Sales Report** task	To open it for editing.
5 Edit the % Complete box to read **25%**	
Press (TAB)	The Status box now displays In Progress.
6 Save the task	It is no longer formatted with strikethrough text; it is not marked as completed.
7 Check the box next to the Analyze Sales Report task	To mark it as completed.
8 View the completed task	⌇ ☑ ~~Analyze Sales Report~~ ⌇ ☐ Create Sales Presentation The checkmark and strikethrough indicate that the task has been completed.

Switching task views

Explanation

Objective 6.1.9

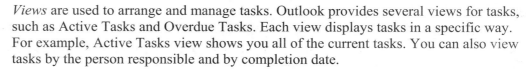

Views are used to arrange and manage tasks. Outlook provides several views for tasks, such as Active Tasks and Overdue Tasks. Each view displays tasks in a specific way. For example, Active Tasks view shows you all of the current tasks. You can also view tasks by the person responsible and by completion date.

To switch to a different view, you select it from the Change View list in the Current View group on the Home tab, as shown in Exhibit 5-4.

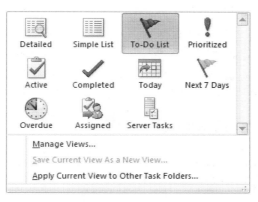

Exhibit 5-4: Task views

Do it!

A-6:   Viewing tasks

Objective 6.1.9

Here's how	Here's why
1 Click **Tasks**	(If necessary.) In the Navigation pane.
2 In the Current View group, click **Change View**	(If necessary.) To display the view options.
3 Click **Detailed**	This view includes the status, due date, and more information.
4 Explore each of the other views	You might have to click Change View or click the More button to see buttons for the other views.
5 Switch to Simple List view	

Topic B: Managing tasks

This topic covers the following Microsoft Office Specialist exam objectives for Outlook 2010.

#	Objective
1.1	**Apply and manipulate Outlook program options**
	1.1.4 Set Task options
	1.5.5 Print tasks
6.1	**Create and manipulate tasks**
	6.1.3 Send a status report
	6.1.5 Move or copy a task to another folder
	6.1.6 Assign a task to another Outlook user
	6.1.7 Accept or decline a task assignment
	6.1.8 Update an assigned task

Explanation

If you're working on a team project, you might need to assign a task to someone else on the team. It might be a task that you cannot finish or one that is more suited to another person. You can create the task and then assign it to someone else by sending a *task request* in an e-mail message. The recipient can accept or decline a task request. If the recipient accepts the task, it's added to the recipient's task list, and the recipient becomes the new owner of the task.

Assigning tasks

Objective 6.1.6

When you assign a task, you might want to track its status. You can do this by keeping an updated copy of the task in your task list and by asking for a status report when the task is completed.

You can also keep a project team updated on your tasks. While you are working on a task, you can send status reports to team members.

To assign a task:

1 Open a task or create a new one.
2 In the Manage Task group on the Task tab, click the Assign Task button.
3 In the To box, enter the e-mail address of the person to whom you want to assign the task.
4 If you want to keep a copy of the task, check "Keep an updated copy of this task on my task list."
5 To be notified when the recipient marks the task as completed, check "Send me a status report when this task is complete."
6 Click Send.

Do it!

B-1:   Assigning a task

Here's how	Here's why
1 Create a task with the subject **xx: Update Sales Web site**	Where *xx* is your partner's lab station number. You'll assign the task of updating the Sales Web site to your partner.
2 From the Start date list, select the first Tuesday of the next month	
From the Due date list, select the last Tuesday of the next month	
3 Click **Details**	(In the Show group on the Task tab.) To display the Details options.
Edit the Total work box to read **200 hours**	To specify the total time needed for the task.
4 Click **Assign Task**	(In the Manage Task group on the Task tab.) The To box and a Send button appear in the Task window.
Address the message to your partner	
5 Verify that **Keep an updated copy of this task on my task list** is checked	When the assignee accepts the task, the task will be moved to that person's Tasks folder and you'll retain a copy of it.
6 Verify that **Send me a status report when this task is complete** is checked	To specify that you want to receive a message when the task is completed.
7 Click **Send**	To send the task request message to your partner. The task is shown with the others in your task list.
8 Check your messages	(View your Inbox.) The task assignment should be listed in your Inbox.

Accepting or declining assigned tasks

Explanation

Objective 6.1.7

If you send a task request to someone and he or she accepts it, the task is no longer yours. The recipient becomes the temporary owner of the task. When the recipient accepts the task, a message appears in your Inbox, stating that the task request has been accepted and ownership passes to the person who accepted the task.

To accept a task request:

1 Open or preview the task request e-mail message.
2 Click Accept.
3 Send a message that informs the sender that you are accepting the task.

When you accept a task, it will appear in your To-Do Bar's Task list.

To decline a task request:

1 Open or preview the task request e-mail message.
2 Click Decline.
3 Send a message that informs the sender that you are declining the task.

If you are the creator a task that is declined, you'll receive a message stating that the task request has been declined. To become the owner of the declined task, open it and click Return to Task List in the Manage Task group on the Ribbon.

Delegating assigned tasks

Objective 6.1.7

There might be occasions when you are assigned a task that someone else is better suited to handle. In that case, you can *delegate,* or send, the task to someone else. When the recipient accepts the task, he or she owns it.

To delegate a task:

1 Open the task request that you want to delegate.
2 In the Manage Task group on the Task tab, click Assign Task.
3 In the To box, enter the new recipient's name.
4 Check or clear the desired options to keep a copy of the task in your Tasks folder and/or to receive a status report when the task is complete.
5 Click Send.

Task folders

When you have multiple tasks, it can be easier to keep track of them by grouping related tasks into a single folder. For example, if you have several tasks related to a business trip, you can create a folder and move or copy the tasks to that folder so all tasks for the trip are together and easy to track.

To create a folder to organize tasks:

1 In the Folder List pane, right-click Tasks and choose New Folder.
2 Name the folder and click OK.
3 In the Task list, select the tasks you want to move to the folder, and drag them to the folder in the Folder List pane.

Do it!

B-2:   Accepting and declining a task request

Here's how	Here's why
1 Open the Inbox folder	(If necessary.) Activate the Mail pane and click Inbox.
2 Select the **Task Request: *yy*: Update Sales Web site** message	Where *yy* is your student number.
3 Observe the Accept and Decline buttons	✓ Accept | ✗ Decline These buttons are shown at the top of the message preview in the Reading pane.
4 Double-click the **Task Request: *yy*: Update Sales Web site** message	To open it.
Observe the Accept and Decline buttons	There are also Accept and Decline buttons in the Respond group on the Ribbon.
5 Click **Accept**	To accept the task.
Verify that **Send the response now** is selected	
Click **OK**	To accept the task and notify the sender that you are accepting it.
6 In the Navigation pane, click **Tasks**	To verify that the task now appears in your Tasks folder. The task you created and assigned to your partner is also listed—that task has your partner's number in the subject.
7 In the Folder List pane, right-click **Tasks** and choose **New Folder...**	
Name the folder **Web Site Work** and click **OK**	The new folder is created below the Tasks folder.
8 Right-click the **Update Sales Web site** task that was sent to you, and hold down the right mouse button	
Drag the task to the Web Site Work folder and choose **Copy**	To copy the task to the new folder. You can now keep tasks related to the Web site together in one location.

9	Click **Change View** and choose **Assigned**	(Or click the More button and click Assigned.) To view tasks in your list that have been assigned to other people.
	Click **Change View** and choose **Simple List**	
10	Create a task with the subject *xx*: **Sales meeting agenda**	Where *xx* is your partner's number.
	Click **Assign Task**	You'll assign the task to your partner.
	Address and send the task to your partner	
11	View your Inbox	
12	Select the **Task Request:** *yy*: **Sales meeting agenda** message	Or open it.
	Click **Decline**	To decline the task.
	Select **Edit the response before sending**	To be able to enter a message about why you are declining the task.
	Click **OK**	
13	In the message area, enter **I will be on vacation next week.**	
	Click **Send**	
14	Check for task response messages	

Declined by Student02 on 2/22/2010 3:06 PM.

Subject:	02: Sale meeting agenda
Due date:	None
Status:	Not Started Priority:
Owner:	Student01

I will be on vacation next week.

Status reports

Explanation

Objectives 6.1.3, 6.1.8

Often you must notify others, such as team members or your manager, of your progress on a task. Outlook provides a couple of ways for you to do this. The most appropriate way to send a status report is to open the task and click Send Status Report in the Manage Task group on the Task tab.

You can also attach the task to an e-mail message or forward the task as an e-mail message. When you're composing a message, tasks are one of the items you can select from the Attach Item list. With a task selected in the Tasks folder, you can click Forward in the Respond group on the Ribbon to forward the task as an e-mail message. Forwarding a task does not reassign it to the recipient.

Do it!

Objectives 6.1.3, 6.1.8

B-3: Sending a task status report

Here's how	Here's why
1 Display the Task list	In the Navigation pane, click Tasks.
Change to Simple List view	
2 Edit the *yy*: **Update Sales Web site** task	Double-click the task assigned to you by your partner.
Set the % Complete to **25%**	You don't have to save your change yet.
3 Click **Send Status Report**	A Message window opens. The Subject line is completed for you, and details of the task are entered into the message body.
Observe the To box	Because this task was assigned to you by your partner, his or her address is already filled in. If this were a task you created, you would have to enter the recipient's address.
In the message area, enter **Change list created.**	A message is optional because the task details are already in the message body.
Press ⏎ ENTER	To move to the next line.
4 Click **Send**	To send the message to your partner.
5 Save the task	Click Save & Close.
6 In the Navigation pane, click **Mail**	To view your Inbox.
7 Select the message	-----Original Task----- **Subject:** 02: Update Sales Web site **Priority:** Normal **Start date:** Tue 3/2/2010 **Due date:** Tue 3/30/2010 **Status:** In Progress **% Complete:** 25% **Actual work:** 0 hours **Requested by:** Student01

Tracking tasks

You might want to receive a confirmation when an assigned task is completed. You track the completion of assigned tasks by using the "Send me a status report when this task is complete" option.

To track a completed task:

1 Create a task.

2 Assign the task.

3 Check "Send me a status report when this task is complete."

4 Send the task request.

When the task is marked completed by the recipient, you'll receive an e-mail notification.

B-4: Tracking an assigned task

Here's how	Here's why
1 Activate Tasks	
2 In the list of tasks, check the box next to the *yy:* **Update Sales Web site** task	To mark the task as completed. Alternatively, you can open the task, change the % Complete to 100%, and save your changes.
3 Activate Mail	
Observe the Task Completed message	-----Original Task----- **Subject:** 02: Update Sales Web site **Priority:** Normal **Start date:** Tue 3/2/2010 **Due date:** Tue 3/30/2010 **Status:** Completed **% Complete:** 100% **Date completed:** Mon 2/22/2010 **Actual work:** 0 hours **Requested by:** Student01

Task options

Explanation

Objective 1.1.4

All tasks have several predefined settings, which you can modify by using the Outlook Options dialog box, shown in Exhibit 5-5. The options are described in the following table.

Option	Use to...
Set reminders on tasks with due dates	Automatically set reminders for a specified time when a task has a due date. Disabled by default.
Keep my task list updated with copies of tasks I assign to other people	Track tasks that you've assigned. Enabled by default.
Send status report when I complete an assigned task	Automatically send a status report when you complete an assigned task. Enabled by default.
Overdue task color; Completed task color	Select colors for tasks that are overdue or completed. The default colors are red (overdue) and gray (completed).
Set Quick Click flag	Set the type of flag to be used when you click in the flag column in your Inbox. By default, the flag type is set to Today.
Task working hours per day	Set your regular workday length. The default is 8 hours.
Task working hours per week	Set your regular workweek length. The default is 40 hours.

To open the Outlook Options dialog box and display the task options, click the File tab and click Options. In the left pane of the Outlook Options dialog box, click Tasks.

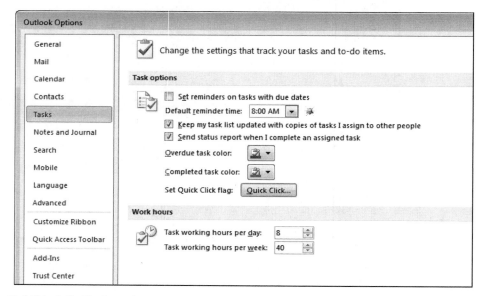

Exhibit 5-5: Task options

B-5: Setting task options

Here's how	Here's why
1 Click the **File** tab and click **Options**	To open the Outlook Options dialog box.
In the left pane, click **Tasks**	To display the task options.
2 Observe the options	The options you set here apply to all tasks.
3 Set a new color for overdue tasks	Select any color in the box.
4 Change your daily working hours to **10**	You can select the text and enter 10, or you can use the arrows to scroll up to 10.
Change your work week to **50** hours	
5 Click **OK**	To close the dialog box and set the options.

Printing tasks

You can print tasks just like you print messages. On the File tab, click Print, and use the print options to print one task or multiple tasks. As with messages, you can print in Table Style, which lists all tasks, or Memo Style, which prints a single task. You can also print a single task by right-clicking it in the Task list and choosing Quick Print.

B-6: Printing tasks

Here's how	Here's why
1 Select a task	
Click the **File** tab and click **Print**	
2 Observe the print styles	You can print all tasks or just a single task.
3 Click the **Home** tab	
4 Right-click a task and choose **Quick Print**	To print the task with the default settings.
5 Close any open windows	

Unit summary: Tasks

Topic A In this topic, you learned that an Outlook task is an activity that must be completed in a specified period of time. You used the **Tasks folder** and the To-Do Bar's **Task list** to add and edit a task. Next, you created a **recurring task** by specifying the recurrence pattern and the range of recurrence. You marked a task as completed. You also learned how to use the different **Task views**.

Topic B In this topic, you **assigned** a task to another person. You also accepted, declined, and delegated **task requests**. In addition, you sent a **status report** for an assigned task. You also **tracked** the completion of an assigned task, set task options, and printed tasks.

Independent practice activity

In this activity, you'll create a task and modify it to be a recurring task. You'll assign a task and track its completion. You'll also accept a task request and mark a task as completed.

1 Create a task with the subject *XX*: **Prepare Web usage report**, where *XX* is your partner's number. Specify the start date as the first working day of the next month, and specify the due date as 10 days after the start date.

2 Save and close the task.

3 Change the Task view to Detailed List.

4 Edit the new task to make it a recurring task. Specify the Recurrence pattern as weekly. The task must recur every Wednesday.

5 Assign the task to your partner. Track the completion of the task.

6 Accept the task request from your partner. Print the task.

7 Mark the task as completed.

Review questions

1 How do you create a task?

Answers can include:

- *In the Navigation pane, click Tasks to display the Tasks pane, and click the New Task button.*

- *With the Tasks pane active, enter a task title in the "Type a new task" box in the Folder pane.*

- *Enter a task name in the "Type a new task" box in the To-Do Bar.*

- *Flag an e-mail message as a task.*

2 How can you assign a task to someone else?

Create or edit a task, and click the Assign Task button on the Task tab.

3 Who is allowed to edit a task?

The task owner is the only person who can edit a task.

4 Which of the following is the term that Outlook uses to describe a task that needs to be performed on a regular basis?

   A Scheduled

   B Repeating

   C Recurring

   D Frequent

5 Name two ways to mark a task as completed.

   Answers can include any of the following:

   • *In the Folder Contents list, select the task and click Mark Complete on the Home tab.*

   • *In the Folder Contents list or the To-Do Bar's Task list, right-click the task and choose Mark Complete.*

   • *Open the task and enter "100%" in the % Complete box.*

   • *Open the task and select Completed from the Status list.*

   • *In Tasks view, check the checkbox next to the task name.*

6 True or false? When a task is marked as completed, it appears in the Tasks view list and the To-Do Bar's Task list with a strikethrough line.

   False. The task appears only in the Tasks view list with the strikethrough line. The task is removed from the To-Do Bar's Task list.

7 True or false? You can set the % Complete for a task only in increments of 25%.

   False. Using the spinners, you can quickly set the percent complete in increments of 25%. You can enter any percent between 0 and 100 by typing the number.

8 When a task request is declined, who owns the task?

   The recipient of the task request has temporary ownership of the task, but after the task has been declined, the task creator can reclaim ownership by opening the task and clicking Return to Task List.

9 Describe the procedure for sending a status report on a task.

   Open the assigned task. Change the status and add information as needed on the Details screen. Click Send Status Report on the Task tab, and send the report.

Unit 6

Appointments and events

Unit time: 50 minutes

Complete this unit, and you'll know how to:

A Use the Calendar to set up and view single and recurring appointments.

B Modify, delete, and restore appointments.

C Add one-time and recurring events.

D Change Calendar views, customize the Calendar, add holidays to the Calendar, and print Calendars.

Topic A: Creating and sending appointments

This topic covers the following Microsoft Office Specialist exam objectives for Outlook 2010.

#	Objective
5.1	**Create and manipulate appointments and events**
	5.1.1 Set appointment options
	5.1.3 Forward an appointment
	5.1.4 Schedule a meeting with a message sender

Explanation

You can use Outlook's Calendar to set up appointments and organize your schedules. You can specify how much of your schedule you want to view at once. The Calendar interface consists of the Calendar pane, the Calendar view, and the Daily Task list, as shown in Exhibit 6-1. There are various Calendar views, including Day, Week, and Month. Day view, the default, displays the selected day in one-hour increments.

The Daily Task list appears in the Day, Work Week, and Week views. This list displays your tasks for the selected day or for each day of the selected week.

Calendar pane   Calendar view   Daily Task list

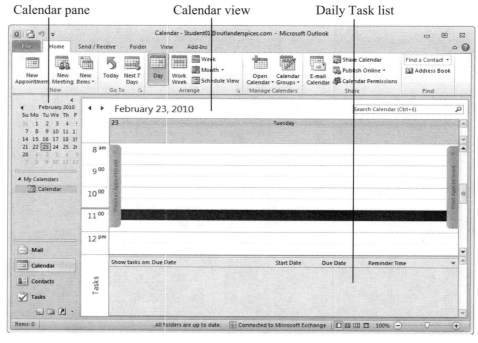

Exhibit 6-1: The Calendar interface

Do it!   **A-1: Exploring the Calendar**

Here's how	Here's why
1 In the Navigation pane, click **Calendar**	
2 Observe the Home tab	Calendar-specific buttons are now available.
3 Observe the Calendar view	It shows the current day divided into one-hour increments. A dark yellow line indicates the current hour. The Daily Task list is shown at the bottom of the view.
4 In the Calendar pane, observe the Date Navigator	By default, it shows the dates for the current month. You can use the arrows in the Date Navigator to move to other months.
5 Observe the My Calendars heading	By default, you see only your calendar. If you were granted access to a co-worker's calendar, it would be listed as well.

Creating appointments

Explanation

Objective 5.1

In Outlook terminology, an *appointment* is a time slot that you reserve on your calendar. You don't invite other people to participate in an appointment. Contrast that to a *meeting*, which does involve other people.

More precisely, an appointment doesn't include any attendees who participate in your Outlook calendaring system. A meeting does involve such people. For example, a doctor appointment would be an appointment, not a meeting, because your doctor doesn't participate in your Outlook calendar, even if she uses Outlook to schedule her time. A scheduled discussion with a co-worker would be a meeting because he does use the same Outlook calendaring system to manage his time.

Appointments don't have to involve anyone other than you. Time you set aside to work on a project would be scheduled on your calendar as an appointment.

There are several ways to create an appointment:

- On the Home tab, click New Appointment. The appointment's start time will be set to the next half-hour time slot.

- On the Home tab, click New Items and choose Appointment. The appointment's start time will be set to the next half-hour time slot.

- Double-click the time slot during which your appointment should be scheduled. The appointment's start time will be set to the time slot you double-clicked.

- Right-click the time slot during which your appointment should be scheduled and choose New Appointment. The appointment's start time will be set to the time slot you right-clicked.

Any of the preceding methods opens the Appointment window, shown in Exhibit 6-2. Here, you specify the subject, location, time, and duration of the appointment.

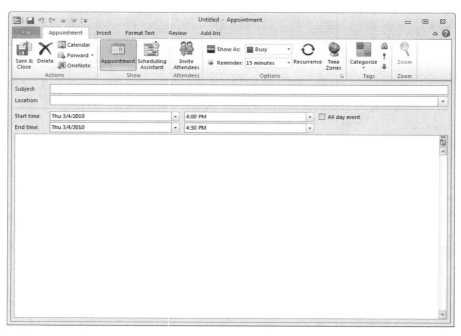

Exhibit 6-2: Creating an appointment

Keep in mind that an appointment does not include a recipient list. If you click the Invite Attendees button on the Appointment tab, you will create a meeting rather than an appointment.

You can specify several options by using the Options group on the Appointment tab. You can use the Show As list to specify your availability status, which can be Free, Tentative, Busy, or Out of Office. Each status has a color associated with it. You can also set a reminder for the appointment. To save the appointment, click Save & Close. After you create and save an appointment, it appears in your Calendar view and in the To-Do Bar.

Marking an appointment as private

Objective 5.1.1

You can mark an appointment as private to prevent other people from accessing the details of your appointments, contacts, or tasks. To ensure that other people cannot read the items you mark as private, do not grant them Read permission to your Calendar, Contacts, or Tasks folders. To mark an appointment as private, click the lock button in the Tags group.

Forwarding appointments

Objective 5.1.3

You can forward an appointment to other people, and they can copy the appointment to their calendars. To forward an appointment, either right-click it in the calendar and choose Forward, or click Forward on the Calendar Tools | Appointment tab. Address the message as you would any new e-mail message, and click Send.

If you receive a forwarded appointment, open the message and double-click the appointment. If you want to add the appointment to your calendar, click "Copy to My Calendar" in the Actions group on the Appointment tab.

Do it!

Objective 5.1

TIPS✓ *Tell students they can also press Ctrl+N.*

A-2: Setting up an appointment

Here's how	Here's why
1 Click **New Appointment**	
	To open a new Appointment window.
2 In the Subject box, enter **Project Research**	To specify the purpose of the appointment.
3 In the Location box, enter **Research Library**	
4 From the Start time list, select tomorrow's date	To specify the start date for the appointment. By default, the end date is the same as the start date.
From the list next to the Start time list, select **10:00 AM**	To specify the start time for the appointment. The end time appears as 30 minutes from the start time.
From the list next to the End time list, select **12:00 PM**	To specify an end time two hours after the start time.
Observe the text area under the End time lists	You can enter any additional comments here.
5 From the Show As list, select **Out Of Office**	(In the Options group on the Appointment tab.) So that your calendar shows that you will be out of the office for this appointment.
6 From the Reminder list, select **30 minutes**	(In the Options group on the Appointment tab.) You'll receive audible and visual notifications 30 minutes before the appointment.
7 Click **Save & Close**	To save the appointment and close the Appointment window. The Next Appointment button in the Calendar view becomes active.
8 Click as shown	
	The calendar for tomorrow is shown, with the time of your appointment.
9 In the Date Navigator, click today's date	To return to today's date.

Objective 5.1.3

10 Right-click the **Project Research** appointment and choose **Forward**

Enter your partner's e-mail address, and click **Send**

11 When you receive the forwarded appointment message, open it

Double-click the appointment attachment and observe the Ribbon

You could click Copy to My Calendar if you wanted to add this appointment to your calendar. For now, though, you'll just close the appointment.

12 Close the appointment and the message from your partner

Adding recurring appointments

Explanation

Objective 5.1.1

Appointments that occur regularly are known as *recurring appointments*. For example, let's say you need to submit expenses monthly. You could schedule a recurring appointment near the end of each month to prepare your expense report.

Create a recurring appointment by using the same techniques you use to create a one-time appointment. Before saving, click Recurrence in the Options group on the Appointment tab. Specify the details of the recurrence by using the Appointment Recurrence dialog box, shown in Exhibit 6-3. Click OK to save those details, and then click Save & Close to save your appointment.

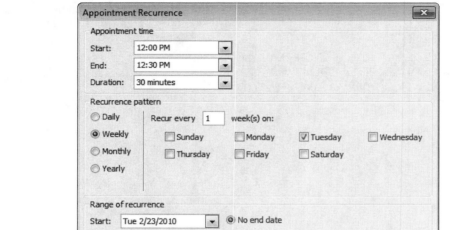

Exhibit 6-3: The Appointment Recurrence dialog box

Do it!

Objective 5.1.1

A-3:   Adding a recurring appointment

Here's how	Here's why
1 Click **New Appointment**	(In Calendar view.)
2 In the Subject box, enter **Expense report**	
3 Set the Start time as the last Wednesday of the month at 3:00 PM Set the End time to 30 minutes after the start time	
4 In the Options group on the Appointment tab, click **Recurrence**	To open the Appointment Recurrence dialog box.
Observe the Start, End, and Duration boxes	You can set these values here rather than when creating the appointment.
5 Under Recurrence pattern, configure the recurrence as shown	

Tell students that their listed dates might be different, depending on what month it is.

Recurrence pattern	
○ Daily	○ Day [24] of every [1] month(s)
○ Weekly	◉ The [last ▼] [Wednesday ▼] of every [1] month(s)
◉ Monthly	
○ Yearly	

6 Observe the "Range of recurrence" section	You would use this portion of the dialog box to set the starting and ending dates for the recurrence.
7 Click **OK**	To close the Appointment Recurrence dialog box.
8 Click **Save & Close**	
9 In the Arrange group on the Home tab, click **Month**	To switch to the monthly view of your calendar. Your recurring appointment is shown on the last Wednesday of the month.

The actual month will vary.

Click the Forward arrow, as shown	◀ ▶ February 2010 Forward Jan 31 Feb 1
	To move to the next month. Your recurring appointment is also listed for this month.

Creating appointments from e-mail messages

Explanation

Objective 5.1.4

You can create an appointment from an e-mail message by dragging it to the Calendar folder. The Appointment window will open, giving you the opportunity to enter necessary details. The original message will be added as an attachment to the appointment.

For example, let's say your co-worker sends you a note about an interesting seminar and you decide to attend. Creating an appointment from the e-mail message reduces clutter in your Inbox while keeping the message accessible in case you need to refer to it later.

There's another way to create an appointment from an e-mail message. While previewing the message, or while it's open, click Move on the Ribbon and choose Calendar. The Appointment window will open so that you can enter necessary details.

Do it!

Objective 5.1.4

A-4: Creating an appointment from an e-mail message

Here's how	Here's why
1 Switch to the Mail folder	
2 Compose an e-mail message to your partner, with these details:	

> Send
>
> Subject: Spice seminar
>
> I thought you might be interested in this seminar.
> It will be held next Tuesday at the XYZ University Auditorium.
>
> **History of Spices**
> By Dr. Basil Rosemary
>
> Uncover hidden facts and the rich details of spices and their impacts on the early development of society.

Here's how	Here's why
Send the message	
3 When your partner's message arrives in your Inbox, open or preview it	It might take a moment to arrive in your Inbox.
4 On the Ribbon, in the Move group, click **Move** and choose **Other Folder ...**	
Select **Calendar** and click **OK**	An Appointment window opens. The subject line is filled in and the e-mail message is attached. You'll need to enter the other details.
5 In the Location box, enter **XYZ University Auditorium**	

6 Enter next Tuesday at **9:00 AM**
   as the Start time

   Enter **11:30 AM** as the End time

7 Click **Save & Close**

8 Observe your Inbox   The e-mail message is gone.

9 View next week on your Calendar   The seminar is listed for next Tuesday.

10 Double-click the **Spice**   To open it.
   Seminar appointment

   Double-click the attachment   Outlook has not deleted the original e-mail
                                             message, but has attached it to the appointment
                                             record.

   Close the Message and   To return to the Calendar.
   Appointment windows

Topic B: Modifying appointments

This topic covers the following Microsoft Office Specialist exam objectives for Outlook 2010.

#	Objective
5.1	**Create and manipulate appointments and events**
	5.1.1 Set appointment options

Explanation

After you create an appointment, you might need to reschedule or cancel it. You can cancel an appointment by deleting it. You can also restore a deleted appointment.

Rescheduling appointments

Objective 5.1.1

You can reschedule an appointment by changing the date, time, location, or other details. To edit an appointment:

1 Double-click the appointment to open it.
2 Make the necessary changes.
3 Click Save & Close.

You can also reschedule appointments by dragging them. With this method, it's easiest to change the date of an appointment in Month view. To drag an appointment to a new time on the same day, use Day view.

B-1: Editing an appointment's text

Objective 5.1.1

Here's how	Here's why
1 Display the calendar in Month view	(In the Navigation pane, click Calendar. On the Home tab, click Month.) You're going to reschedule the Project Research appointment.
On the Home tab, click **Today**	
2 Double-click the **Project Research** appointment	(In the calendar grid or in the To-Do Bar.) To open the Appointment window.
3 Change the start date and the end date to one day later	To postpone the appointment by one day.
Edit the Location box to read **Research Library, Building K**	
4 In the text area, type the indicated text	1. Spice origins 2. Trade agreements with Malaysia
5 Save the appointment	The appointment is postponed by one day.
6 Point to the appointment	25 26 27 Project Research; 10:00 AM - 12:00 PM Project Research (Research Library, Building K) The tooltip shows details of the appointment.
7 Drag the appointment back to its original day	You can change the date of an appointment by dragging it in Month view.
8 Change to Day view	Click Day on the Ribbon.
9 Drag the appointment so it starts at 11:00 AM	You can change the time of an appointment by dragging it in Day view.

Help students find the appointment.

TIPS *Tell students that they can also change the time of an appointment by dragging it to another time slot in the calendar grid.*

Rescheduling recurring appointments

Explanation

⌐

Objective 5.1.1

If you want to modify a recurring appointment, here's how:

1 Double-click the appointment to open the Open Recurring Item dialog box.
2 If you want to modify a single occurrence, select "Open this occurrence." If you want to modify all occurrences of the recurring appointment, select "Open the series."
3 Click OK to open the Appointment window.
4 Click Recurrence in the Options group on the Appointment tab.
5 Make the necessary changes and click OK.
6 Click Save & Close.

Do it!

Objective 5.1.1

B-2: Modifying a recurring appointment

Here's how	Here's why
1 Switch to Month view	
2 Double-click the **Expense Report** appointment	To display the Open Recurring Item dialog box. You can modify either the selected occurrence or all occurrences of the recurring appointment.
3 Select **Open the series**	You'll change all occurrences of this recurring appointment.
Click **OK**	To open the Appointment window.
4 Click **Recurrence**	(In the Options group on the Appointment tab.) To open the Appointment Recurrence dialog box.
Under Appointment time, from the Start list, select **11:30 AM**	
Change the appointment to occur on the last Monday of every month, as shown	

◉ The	last ▾	Monday ▾	of every	1	month(s)

Under "Range of recurrence," set the start date to today's date	For a recurring appointment, the range does not need to begin on the date of the first appointment.
Click **OK**	
5 Save and close the appointment	
6 Observe the calendar	(In Month view.) The appointment has moved to the last Monday of the month. If today is after the last Monday of the month, the event will not be visible. You'll have to view the next month to see it.

Deleting and restoring appointments

Explanation

You can delete appointments that are no longer needed or that have been canceled. To delete an appointment, select it and click the Delete button on the Ribbon. You can also press the Delete key or press Ctrl+D.

You can restore a deleted appointment. If you haven't done anything else since deleting the appointment, you can press Ctrl+Z to undo the deletion. Until you empty the Deleted Items folder, you can restore the appointment from there. You can drag it back to the Calendar folder, or right-click the item and choose Move, Calendar.

Do it!

B-3:   Deleting and restoring an appointment

Here's how	Here's why
1 On the Ribbon, click **Today**	If necessary, to return to this month and highlight today's date on the calendar.
2 Select the **Project Research** appointment	You'll delete this appointment.
3 Click **Delete**	![Delete button] To delete the appointment.
4 Press CTRL + Z	To undo the deletion.
5 Press DELETE	To delete the appointment again.
6 Click ⬚	(At the bottom of the Navigation pane.) To display the folder list.
Select **Deleted Items**	
7 Right-click the **Project Research** appointment	Student01 11:40 AM Project Research In the folder list.
Click **Move** and choose **Calendar**	To move the item back to the Calendar.
8 Activate the Calendar	The appointment has been restored.
9 Delete the Project Research appointment	Select it, and then either click Delete or press the Delete key.

Topic C: Working with events

This topic covers the following Microsoft Office Specialist exam objectives for Office 2010.

#	Objective
5.1	Create and manipulate appointments and events
	5.1.1 Set appointment options

Explanation

In Outlook, an *event* is an activity that lasts for a period of one or more days and that can be added to the Calendar. There are three types of events in Outlook: single-day, multi-day, and recurring. For example, workshops, conferences, and seminars can be single- or multi-day events. Birthdays and anniversaries are examples of events that recur annually. Quarterly tax filing deadlines are an example of events that recur on something other than an annual basis. By default, Outlook assumes that events last for at least one day. However, you can change this setting and specify the duration of an event.

Single- and multi-day events

You can add single-day and multi-day events to the Calendar. Here's how:

Objective 5.1.1

1   On the Home tab, in the New group, click New Items and choose All Day Event to open a new Event window. (You can also create an appointment and check the "All day event" box, next to the End times boxes, in the Appointment window.)

2   Specify the subject and location for the event.

3   Do one of the following:

- If it is a single-day event that runs for the entire day, select the same date for the start and end dates. "All day event" is checked by default.

- If it is a multi-day event, select the start and end dates.

4   From the Show As list on the Event tab, select the status you want shown on your Calendar. For birthday or anniversary events, you should select Free. The other status types would be more appropriate for classes, seminars, and trips.

5   Use the Reminder list on the Event tab to specify when you want to be reminded about the event.

6   Click Save & Close to save the event and close the Event window.

Marking an event as private

You can mark an event as private to prevent other people from accessing the details of your personal events. To mark an event as private, open it and click Private in the Options group on the Event tab.

Creating events from messages and tasks

You can also create events from messages and tasks. To do so, drag the e-mail message or task to the Calendar folder. The Appointment window will open. Enter the necessary details and click Save & Close.

Do it!

Objective 5.1.1

C-1: Adding an event

Here's how	Here's why
1 Switch to Month view	If necessary.
2 Click **New Items** and choose **All Day Event**	(In the New group on the Home tab.) To open a new Event window.
3 In the Subject box, enter **Medicinal spice seminar**	
4 Specify the start date as the first Monday of the next month	Use the Date Navigator to advance to the next month.
5 Specify the end date as the date that is two working days after the start date	
6 From the Show As list, select **Out of Office**	
Observe the Reminder list	The default reminder is set for 18 hours before the event.
7 Click **Save & Close**	To save the event and close the Event window.
8 View the first Monday of next month	(Advance to the next month and view the first Monday.) The event appears as a banner across the scheduled days.

Students might have a conflict with the Spice seminar appointment.

Recurring events

Explanation

Objective 5.1.1

Recurring events happen more than once. For example, a birthday happens every year on the same day. Estimated taxes are due every quarter. You create a recurring event by specifying a Recurrence. Here's one way to do this:

1 With the Calendar open, click New Items on the Home tab and choose All Day Event.

2 Enter the event details, such as subject, location, and date.

3 Click Recurrence (in the Options group on the Event tab) to open the Appointment Recurrence dialog box.

4 Under Recurrence pattern, specify when and for how long the event recurs.

5 Click OK.

6 Click Save & Close.

Alternatively, you can:

1 Right-click the appropriate time slot and choose New Recurring Event. For example, in Month view, right-click a day's box to create a recurring event on that date. Both the Event window and the Appointment Recurrence dialog box open.

2 Define the recurrence pattern and click OK.

3 Enter the event details, such as subject, location, and so forth.

4 Click Save & Close.

Do it!

Objective 5.1.1

C-2: Adding an annual event

Here's how	Here's why
1 Click **New Items** and choose **All Day Event**	(In the New group on the Home tab.) To open a new Event window.
Specify the subject as **National Ice Cream Day**	
2 For the Start time, select the third Sunday in July	Depending on the current date, you might notice a message in the InfoBar, telling you that the selected date occurs in the past. Because this event will be changed to an annual one, you can ignore this message.
3 On the Event tab, in the Options group, click **Recurrence**	To open the Appointment Recurrence dialog box.
Under Recurrence pattern, select **Yearly**	

4 Verify that the recurrence period
   is selected as shown

5 Close the Appointment
   Recurrence dialog box

6 Save the event

7 Switch to Month view   If necessary.

8 Navigate to July

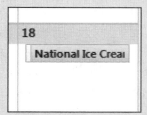

(Use the Date Navigator or the Forward button.)
The event appears on the third Sunday.

9 Press ⌜CTRL⌝ + ⌜G⌝   To open the Go To Date dialog box.

   In the Date box, enter   Where 20## is next year, such as 7/1/2012.
   7/1/20##

   Confirm that **Month Calendar**
   is selected

   Click **OK**   Next year's July is shown. National Ice Cream
                                 Day is shown on the third Sunday.

10 Click **Today**   (On the Ribbon.) To display the current date in
                                 Calendar view.

Topic D: Using Calendar views

This topic covers the following Microsoft Office Specialist exam objectives for Outlook 2010.

#	Objective
1.5	**Print an Outlook item**
	1.5.2 Print Calendars
5.3	**Manipulate the Calendar pane**
	5.3.1 Arrange the Calendar view

Explanation

Outlook provides various Calendar views, including Day, Work Week, Week, Month, and Schedule. To change the view, click the appropriate button on the Ribbon. (Buttons for these views are on the Home tab and the View tab.) You can view as much of your schedule as you want to at a time.

Day view

Objective 5.3.1

Day view, as shown in Exhibit 6-4, shows all of your calendar items for a single day. The current date is selected by default. If you want to view items for another day, click the Forward or Back navigation buttons to the left of the date or use the Date Navigator in the Navigation pane.

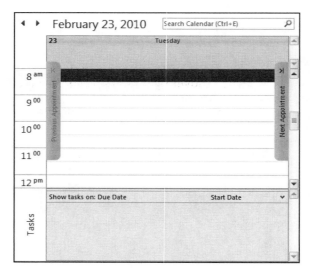

Exhibit 6-4: Day view

Work Week and Week views

Objective 5.3.1

Work Week view displays the current five-day work week, as shown in Exhibit 6-5. If you prefer to view a full seven-day week, click Week to show Week view. Use the Forward and Back buttons to view other weeks, or click a date in the Date Navigator to show that week's items.

Exhibit 6-5: Work Week view

Month view

Objective 5.3.1

Month view, shown in Exhibit 6-6, shows the entire month. The heading of today's date is highlighted in yellow. The box for the date you have selected is shaded in light blue.

Dates in the previous and next months are displayed so that there are no empty boxes in the calendar. But such dates are shown with a darker blue background to indicate that they are not part of the current month.

Exhibit 6-6: Month view

Schedule view

Objective 5.3.1

Schedule view, shown in Exhibit 6-7, is a combined view of all of the calendars you have opened. This view is useful for checking the availability of the members on a team or in a workgroup.

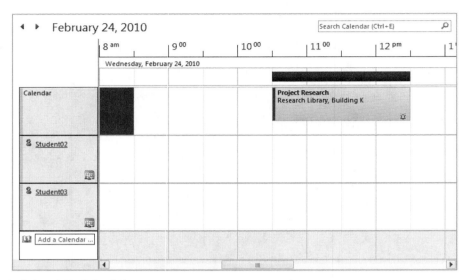

Exhibit 6-7: Schedule view

Do it!

Objective 5.3.1

D-1:   **Exploring Calendar views**

Here's how	Here's why
1 On the Home tab, click **Day**	To switch to Day view.
2 Observe the Calendar view	Day view shows the day's calendar items.
3 Click **Work Week**	(On the Home tab.) The calendar grid displays the current work week, Monday to Friday. Use this view to see the entire work week at a glance.
4 Click **Week**	To show the full seven-day week. Weekend days are shaded blue.
5 Click the top half of the Month button, as shown	
	To view the calendar for the entire month.
Click as shown	
	To display the Month view menu.
Choose **Show Low Detail**	In the low-detail version of Month view, only the day boxes are shown. Calendar items are not visible.
Show Medium details on the Month view	(From the Month view menu, choose Show Medium Detail.) In this view, a line divides each day into morning and afternoon. Calendar items are visible as small gray bars.
Show High details on the Month view	This is the default Month view.
6 Click **Schedule View**	To show today's calendar in Schedule view. If you had multiple calendars open, such as those of a co-worker, you'd see events from all of the calendars listed in this single view.
7 Click **Day**	To return to the default view.

Calendar shortcuts

Explanation

To help you more efficiently use the Calendar, Outlook provides many tricks and shortcuts for accessing frequently used features. Some of these are listed in the following table.

To do this...	Use these shortcuts
Create an appointment	• Double-click a time slot. • In Day view, click the blue band beneath the day's label bar (for example, the bar containing the word "Monday"). • Point to a time slot. When the "Click to add" button appears, click it. • Drag across multiple time slots to select them. Then point to the selected slots. When the "Click to add" button appears, click it.
Switch to Day view	• In any other Calendar view, click the day's label bar. • When viewing another folder, such as Mail, click the date in the Date Navigator.
Switch to Work Week view from Month view	• At the left end of a week's row, click the date range label.

Do it!   **D-2: Exploring Calendar shortcuts**

Here's how	Here's why
1 Point to the blue bar beneath today's label	
	After a moment, it becomes a "Click to add event" button.
2 Point to an empty time slot	
	After a moment, it becomes a "Click to add appointment" button.
3 Switch to Work Week view	
Click tomorrow's label	
	To switch to Day view for tomorrow's calendar.
4 Switch to Month view	
Click the date range label to the left of the current week	
	To switch to Work Week view for this week.

If it's Friday, have students click yesterday's label.

Setting workdays and times

Explanation

The default work week is Monday through Friday, and the work day typically begins at 8:00 AM and ends at 5:00 PM. You might want to change the work days or the times of the day. You can change these calendar settings by using the Calendar page in the Outlook Options dialog box, shown in Exhibit 6-8.

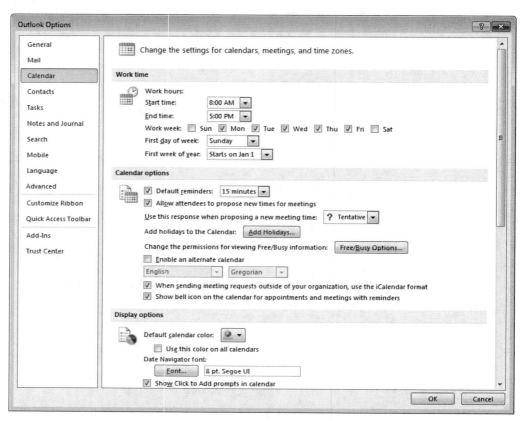

Exhibit 6-8: Calendar settings in the Outlook Options dialog box

Do it!

D-3: Customizing the Calendar

Here's how	Here's why
1 Click the **File** tab and then click **Options**	To open the Outlook Options dialog box.
In the left pane, click **Calendar**	To display Calendar-related options.
2 Under Work hours, change the Start time to **9:00 AM**	To change the work week's start time.
Change the End time to **6:00 PM**	
3 From the "First day of week" list, select **Monday**	To switch to a Monday-to-Sunday week.
4 Click **OK**	To close the Outlook Options dialog box.
5 Switch to Day view	The day now starts at 9:00 AM (the 8:00 AM time slot is shaded blue).
6 Switch to Week view	The week runs from Monday to Sunday.
7 Switch to Month view	The first column is now Monday, not Sunday.

Make sure students choose Week, not Work Week, view.

Displaying multiple time zones

Explanation

You might have business associates or clients who are located around the world. When scheduling activities such as conference calls, you need to consider the time zones for these locations. You can add time zones to schedule your activities more easily.

To display a second time zone:

1 On the File tab, click Options to open the Outlook Options dialog box.

2 In the left pane, click Calendar.

3 In the Time zones section, check "Show a second time zone."

4 (Optional) Enter a label. If you do so, it will be displayed in Day view and other locations where times are displayed.

5 From the Time zone list, select the time zone you want to add.

6 Check or clear "Automatically adjust for daylight savings time" to match the practices of your new locale. (Not all regions observe Daylight Savings Time.)

7 Click OK.

Do it!

D-4: Displaying multiple time zones

Here's how	Here's why
1 Open the Outlook Options dialog box	Click the File tab and click Options.
In the left pane, click **Calendar**	To display Calendar-related options.
2 Under Time zones, check **Show a second time zone**	Scroll down to find this section.
From the second Time zone list, select a time zone other than your local one	For example, if you're in the Eastern time zone, choose the Pacific time zone.
In the Label box, enter **There**	
3 Under Time zones, in the first Label box, enter **Here**	You are using these labels to distinguish between your local and second time zones. At your office, you might use more precise labels, such as Eastern, Mtn, or PST.
4 Click **OK**	To save your changes.
5 Switch to Day view	Both time zones are displayed in Day view, with your local time zone to the right of the secondary time zone.

Holidays

You can display holidays commonly celebrated in your country in the Calendar. Holidays appear on the Calendar as all-day events.

To add the holidays to the Calendar:

1 Open the Outlook Options dialog box, and click Calendar.

2 Under Calendar options, click Add Holidays to open the Add Holidays to Calendar dialog box.

3 In the list of countries, check your country.

4 Click OK. A message states that the holidays are added to your Calendar.

5 Click OK to return to the Outlook Options dialog box.

6 Click OK to close the Outlook Options dialog box.

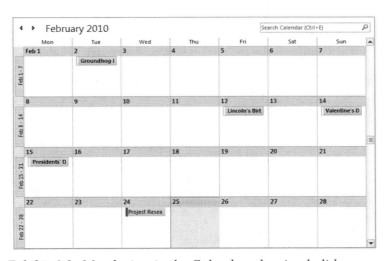

Exhibit 6-9: Month view in the Calendar, showing holidays

Do it!

D-5: Adding holidays to the Calendar

Here's how	Here's why
1 Open the Outlook Options dialog box	
Click **Calendar**	To display Calendar-related options.
2 Under Calendar options, click **Add Holidays**	To open the Add Holidays to Calendar dialog box.
3 Verify that your country is checked	
4 Click **OK**	To import the holidays into your Calendar. A message states that the holidays have been added.
Click **OK**	To return to the Outlook Options dialog box.
5 Click **OK**	To return to the Calendar.
6 Switch to Month view	Holidays are now listed on your Calendar. If no official holidays fall in the current month, view another month.

Printing calendars

Explanation

Objective 1.5.2

There might be times when you want a hard copy of your calendar, such as when you're going to be away from the office and don't have access to your computer. To print your calendar, display the calendar you want to print, click the File tab, and then click Print.

You can print your calendar using one of the following styles:

- **Daily Style** — Prints the daily schedule and includes the daily task list and a section for notes.
- **Weekly Agenda Style** — Includes seven days with a box for each day, with smaller boxes for weekend days. Also includes small versions of the current and next months.
- **Weekly Calendar Style** — Includes all seven days in columns, with hours as rows.
- **Monthly Style** — Prints one full month in a traditional calendar layout.
- **Tri-fold Style** — Prints three "panes": one for today's schedule, one for tasks, and another for the week at a glance.
- **Calendar Details Style** — Prints a list of appointments by day.

To print a calendar, in one of the Calendar views, click the File tab and then click Print. Select the style you want, and click Print.

To print a single appointment, open it, click the File tab, and click Print. To print the appointment and its details in Memo Style, click the Print button. You can also right-click the appointment in the calendar and choose Quick Print.

Do it!

Objective 1.5.2

The Calendar is displayed in Month view.

D-6: Printing a Calendar

Here's how	Here's why
1 Click the **File** tab and click **Print**	To display printing options for the Calendar.
Observe the settings	Because you are in Month view, Monthly Style is the default choice.
2 Select **Daily Style** and observe the preview	It lists today's appointments.
Note the page indicator at the bottom of the preview pane	◀ 1 of 35 ▶ The entire month will print in Daily Style. Like any document, you can print just single pages.
3 Select **Monthly Style** and click **Print**	To print one month of your calendar.
4 Right-click an appointment and choose **Quick Print**	To print a single appointment.
5 Close any open windows	

Unit summary: Appointments and events

Topic A   In this topic, you learned about the **Calendar** and its various views. You added **appointments** by using the Appointment window. You added a recurring appointment, and you learned how to add an appointment from a message or a task.

Topic B   In this topic, you **edited** a regular appointment and a recurring appointment. Then you **deleted** an appointment and **restored** the deleted appointment.

Topic C   In this topic, you added **events** to the Calendar. You added both one-time and recurring events.

Topic D   In this topic, you compared the various Calendar views. You changed the **work-day times** and added a **second time zone** to your Calendar. Then you added a holiday to your Calendar and printed a Calendar.

Independent practice activity

In this activity, you'll create a recurring appointment. You'll view an appointment, delete it, and restore it. In addition, you'll e-mail an appointment and create an annual event.

1 Create an appointment for tomorrow at 9:00 AM. Specify the subject as **Spice Seminar**, the location as **Paradise Theater**, and the end time as 10:30 AM.

2 Change the appointment so that it's recurring, repeating every month for four months. (*Hint:* Under "Range of recurrence," enter the relevant value in the End after box.)

3 Observe the appointment in the various Calendar views. Print the appointment.

4 Delete all occurrences of the Spice Seminar appointment that you scheduled.

5 Set the work day to begin at 8:00 AM and end at 5:00 PM. Set the calendar week to begin on Sunday.

6 Show only a single time zone on your calendar. Remove the label for your local time zone.

Review questions

1 Which of the following can be used to display a different month? [Choose all that apply.]

A The Forward and Back navigation buttons in Month view

B The Current View list

C The Date Navigator

D The Daily Task list

2 What is the difference between an appointment, a meeting, and an event?

An appointment is a scheduled block of time that involves only you or those outside your organization who don't participate in your Outlook Calendaring system.

A meeting is a scheduled time block when you are meeting with others who do participate in your Outlook Calendaring system. You are inviting and managing the meeting attendees.

An event runs for an entire day (or longer), and you can either invite other attendees or not.

3 What is the definition of a recurring appointment?

An appointment that occurs on a daily, weekly, monthly, or yearly basis.

4 How do you create a recurring appointment?

There are two ways to create a recurring appointment.

- *Create an appointment and click Recurrence.*
- *Right-click a time slot and choose New Recurring Appointment.*

5 Which button can you use to quickly display the appointments for the current day?

The Today button

6 What is the procedure to change your calendar so that every day starts at 9:00 AM?

a   On the File tab, click Options to open the Outlook Options dialog box.

b   Click Calendar to show calendar options.

c   Under Work time, from the Start time list, select 9:00 AM.

d   Click OK.

7 You want to add an item to your calendar to mark the date your company was founded. Would you add a meeting, an appointment, or an event?

An event.

8 How many days are shown in the default Week view?

Seven days, starting on Sunday.

9 True or false? When you create an appointment from an e-mail message, you can delete the message so that it doesn't remain in your Inbox.

False. The e-mail message is automatically removed from your Inbox and attached to the appointment.

10 If you delete an appointment and then find that you still need it, how do you restore it to the Calendar?

Move it from the Deleted Items folder to the Calendar folder by dragging it or by using the Ribbon or the right-click shortcut menus.

Unit 7

Meeting requests and responses

Unit time: 50 minutes

Complete this unit, and you'll know how to:

A Use the Calendar to create and send meeting requests, and respond to meeting requests by accepting or declining them or by proposing a new meeting time.

B Reserve resources, manage meeting responses, and update and cancel meetings.

Topic A: Scheduling meetings

This topic covers the following Microsoft Office Specialist exam objectives for Outlook 2010.

#	Objective
5.2	**Create and manipulate meeting requests**
5.2.1	Set response options
5.2.2	Update a meeting request
5.2.3	Cancel a meeting or invitation
5.2.4	Propose a new time for a meeting
5.3	**Manipulate the Calendar pane**
5.3.3	Display or hide calendars

Explanation

Objective 5.2

In Outlook terminology, a *meeting* is a time slot you reserve on your Calendar, as well as on the Outlook Calendar of one or more additional attendees. Contrast that to an *appointment*, which does not involve other people (or involves only people who are not part of your Outlook calendaring system).

For example, if you and your co-worker Sally use Outlook's Calendar tools to coordinate a time to discuss a project, you are creating a meeting. If you schedule a time on your Calendar to visit the dentist, that's an appointment. Even though that time slot involves another person, it's not a meeting because your dentist doesn't use the same Outlook calendaring system to manage his time.

Meeting requests

A *meeting request* is a special type of message that contains all the details of a proposed meeting time. After you create a meeting request, it is sent to all of the participants you invite. Each of them can accept, decline, or suggest an alternate time for the meeting. If your Exchange environment has been set up for it, meeting requests can even book locations and equipment, such as a projector, VCR, computer, and so forth.

Calendaring is such an integral part of Outlook that the program provides many ways to create meeting requests. You will probably find one or two methods you use most often. Even if you don't use them all, it's nice to know that you can create meeting requests by using any of these methods:

- Open the Meeting window and enter the meeting details. You can open a new Meeting window in various ways:
  - In any of the folders (Inbox, Contacts, and so forth), click New Items and choose Meeting.
  - In any Calendar view, click the Meeting button on the Ribbon.
  - In any Calendar view, right-click a time slot and choose New Meeting Request.
  - In any of the folders, press Ctrl+Shift+Q.
- Create an appointment or event, and then click Invite Attendees on the Ribbon. This converts the appointment or event into a meeting.

- Create an appointment or event, and then click Scheduling Assistant on the Ribbon. Add the calendars of all prospective attendees. Double-click the header atop the time slot that is free for all attendees. This converts the appointment or event into a meeting.

- In the Calendar, switch to Schedule view. Add the calendars of all prospective attendees. Double-click the header atop the time slot that is free for all attendees.

- Use drag-and-drop or the menus to move an e-mail message to the Calendar. Using the resulting Appointment window, invite attendees; this converts the appointment into a meeting.

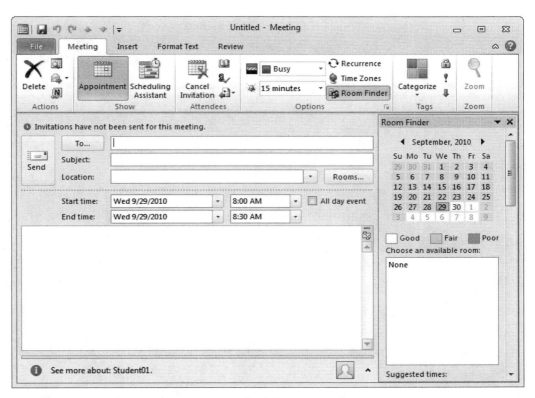

Exhibit 7-1: Create meeting requests in the Meeting window

Response options

To configure response options, click Response Options in the Attendees group on the Ribbon. By default, both options—Request Responses and Allow New Time Proposals—are enabled. To disable one of the options, select it to uncheck it.

Do it!

A-1: Creating and sending a meeting request

Objective 5.2

Make sure students know that they will work in pairs and that one partner will need to add one hour to all of the times printed in the book when scheduling appointments.

Make sure partners use the correct times.

Here's how	Here's why
1 With your partner, decide who will be partner A and who will be partner B	Partner A will schedule appointments, events, and meetings at the times printed in the book. Partner B will schedule items at one hour *after* the times printed in the book.
2 Activate the Calendar	In the Navigation pane, click Calendar.
3 Click **New Meeting**	To open a new Meeting window. The InfoBar tells you that invitations have not been sent for the meeting, and it might warn you that the meeting occurs in the past.
4 In the To box, enter your partner's e-mail address	
In the Subject box, enter **XX: Sales strategy for the Midwest region**	In place of *XX*, use your partner's number.
In the Location box, enter **Conference Room**	To specify the location for the meeting.
5 Use the Start time and End time fields to schedule the meeting for tomorrow from **9:00 AM** to **10:00 AM**	If you're partner B, schedule the meeting for 10:00 AM to 11:00 AM.
6 Observe the Reminder list	(In the Options group on the Meeting tab.) It is set to remind you 15 minutes before the meeting.
In the Show As list, verify that **Busy** is selected	To mark the allocated time as busy in your Calendar. Other options are Free, Tentative, and Out of Office.
7 Click **Response Options**	In the Attendees group.
Observe the settings	You can see that you are requesting responses and allowing proposals for a new time. Both settings are enabled by default.
8 Click **Send**	To send the meeting request and close the Meeting window.

9 Switch to Day view   If necessary.

View tomorrow's schedule

9 00	**02: Sales strategy for the Midwest region** **Conference Room** **Student01**
10 00	01: Sales strategy for the Midwest region Conference Room Student02

(Click the Forward button or click tomorrow's date in the Date Navigator.) The meeting is listed on your Calendar. Your partner's meeting will also be listed (though perhaps not immediately) because he or she invited you.

Meeting requests

Explanation

Meeting requests are delivered to all invitees, and the requests show up in the Inbox just like e-mail messages do. When you preview or open the meeting request, you will be able to see all of the meeting's details, such as the date, time, and location. The meeting request also shows you the relevant portion of your calendar (this feature is new in Outlook 2010) so you can quickly determine whether you can attend the meeting. This feature is shown in Exhibit 7-2.

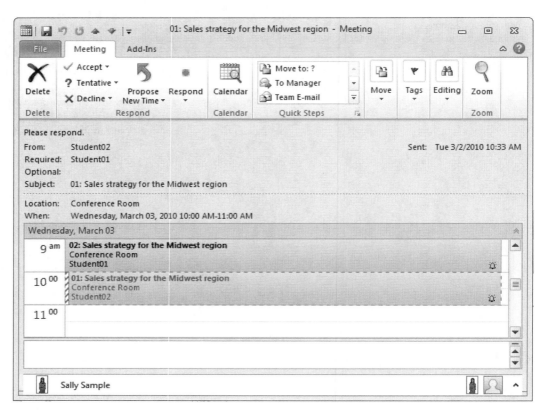

Exhibit 7-2: A Meeting Request window

Outlook provides buttons to enable you to reply to a meeting request. You can click Accept, Tentative, or Propose New Time. If you need to communicate with the meeting organizer, you can click Respond and choose Reply, Reply to All, and so forth. Doing so enables you to send an e-mail message, such as to confirm missing details, without yet accepting or declining the request.

Depending on the action you take, Outlook will update your calendar, as well as the calendar of the organizer. For example, clicking Accept will add a meeting item to your calendar and mark you as attending in the organizer's view of the meeting.

Do it!

A-2: Reading and accepting a meeting request

Here's how	Here's why
1 Activate Mail	
Observe the new message	01: Sales strategy for the ... Student02 10:34 AM
	In the Folder Contents list, the icon to the left of the new message indicates that the message is a meeting request.
2 Select the **YY: Sales strategy for the Midwest region** message	When you preview or open the Meeting window, you have access to additional buttons for checking your calendar, forwarding the request, or deleting it.
Observe the buttons at the top of the preview	✓ Accept ▾ ? Tentative ▾ ✗ Decline ▾ ↳ Propose New Time ▾
Observe the contents of the message	A preview of your calendar is included in the message body. It shows your current schedule for the date and time of this meeting request.
3 Click **Accept**	You're given the choice to edit your response, send the response, or accept the meeting request without sending a response.
Choose **Send the Response Now**	The meeting is added to your calendar, and the request is removed from your Inbox.
4 Observe your Inbox	02: Sales strategy for Midwest... Student02 9:24 PM
	After a moment or two, a meeting acceptance notice from your partner will arrive.
5 Open the message	Accepted: Student01 Tentative: No attendees have tentatively accepted. Declined: No attendees have declined.
	The message header indicates that your partner has accepted your request for a meeting.
6 Close the Meeting Response window	

TIPS ✓ *If students select the message, or if Outlook selects it automatically, the icon will change.*

Displaying and hiding calendars

Explanation

If you need to regularly schedule meetings with a small group of co-workers, you can add their calendars to your Calendar folder. (In fact, for Schedule view to be useful, you must first add the other attendees' calendars to your Calendar folder. Otherwise, Schedule view shows just your calendar.) You won't be able to modify the added calendars, but you'll be able to see your co-workers' availability and use Schedule view to create meeting requests for times that you see are free for all attendees.

Objective 5.3.3

To add a calendar:

1 In any Calendar view, click Open Calendar on the Ribbon and choose the appropriate source. For example, to open the calendar of another user within your Exchange organization, choose From Address Book.

2 Select the calendar or calendars you want to add.

3 Click Calendar.

4 Click OK.

Once you've added a calendar, it will be displayed alongside your calendar in the various views.

To hide a calendar, click the Close button (the ×) on the tab beside the other user's calendar, or uncheck the box next to that person's calendar in the Navigation pane. Doing this does not remove your connection to that person's calendar; it just hides the calendar temporarily. Simply check the box in the Navigation pane to show the calendar again.

To remove a calendar, right-click it in the Navigation pane and choose Delete Calendar.

Viewing other users' calendars and adding them to your Calendar view requires an Exchange Server or third-party components.

Do it!

Objective 5.3.3

A-3: Displaying and hiding calendars

Here's how	Here's why
1 Activate the Calendar	
2 In the Manage Calendars group, click **Open Calendar**	On the Ribbon.
Choose **From Address Book...**	
3 Select your partner	
Click **Calendar ->**	
Click **OK**	You can now see both calendars. Notice the changes in the Navigation pane: both calendars are listed there now.
4 Switch to Day view	If necessary. You see both calendars in a tabbed arrangement.
5 Click **Schedule View**	On the Ribbon.
6 Double-click your partner's schedule under 10:00 AM (Partner B, click under 11:00 AM)	A new Meeting window opens. Your partner's address is entered, as is the time block you selected.
Click **Delete**	(On the Ribbon.) To cancel the operation and not create the meeting request.
7 Switch to Day view	
8 Next to your partner's name, click the **X**	To close your partner's calendar.
Observe the Navigation pane	Your partner's calendar is still listed, but it's unchecked. You have not removed it, but simply hidden it from view.
9 In the Navigation pane, right-click your partner's calendar and choose **Delete Calendar**	It is removed from your Navigation pane. The group, Shared Calendars, remains.
10 Right-click **Shared Calendars** and choose **Delete Group**	
Click **Yes**	To delete the entire group. If it contained calendars, they would also be removed.

Partner B should schedule the meeting at 11:00.

Scheduling meetings

Explanation

Outlook provides tools you can use to check an attendee's schedule before you create your meeting request. You can do this in Schedule view in the Calendar or in the Invite Attendees window.

Objective 5.2

When you need to regularly schedule meetings with an individual, you will probably want to add his or her calendar to your Calendar folder. For those other people with whom you don't regularly schedule meetings, you can use the Scheduling Assistant to check their calendars while scheduling a meeting. Here's how:

1 Open a new Meeting window.
2 Enter pertinent details, such as the subject, location, and date and time.
3 Optionally, enter the attendees in the To box.
4 Click Scheduling Assistant.
5 If you did not add attendees in step 3, then under the All Attendees column, click "Click here to add a name." Enter the attendee's name or e-mail address and press Enter.
6 Highlight a suitable time that is free for all attendees. You can click a column header to select a half-hour block, or drag across multiple columns to schedule longer meetings. Use the Date Navigator to quickly scroll to future dates.
7 Click Send.

You should enter the meeting details, such as the subject, before opening the Scheduling Assistant. But if you open it before entering the details, simply click the Appointment button to return to the Meeting window.

The Scheduling Assistant requires an Exchange Server or third-party components.

Do it!

Objective 5.2

A-4: Scheduling a meeting

Here's how	Here's why
1 Click **New Meeting**	
2 Enter your partner's e-mail address in the To box	
In the Subject box, enter **XX: Product Planning**	Where *XX* is your partner's lab number.
In the Location box, enter **Conference Room**	You must enter meeting details before opening the Scheduling Assistant.
3 Click **Scheduling Assistant**	 To open the Scheduling Assistant. Because you entered your partner's e-mail address, his or her calendar is made available in the Assistant. You could add others.
4 Scroll to show tomorrow's schedule	You have already scheduled a meeting with your partner for tomorrow morning at 9:00. This time is blocked out on the schedule.

Partner B should schedule the appointment for 2:00.

5 Click where indicated

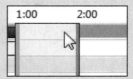

(On the gray heading under 1:00 PM tomorrow.) To select the 1:00-to-1:30 PM half-hour slot.

6 Click again in the same spot and drag to the right

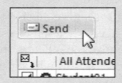

To select the whole 1:00 hour.

7 Click **Send**

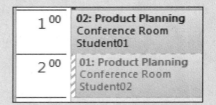

To send the meeting request to your partner.

Remind students that it might take a moment for their partner's meeting to appear on their calendar.

8 View tomorrow's schedule in Day view

1 00	**02: Product Planning** Conference Room Student01
2 00	**01: Product Planning** Conference Room Student02

The newly proposed meeting is shown.

Declining meeting requests

Explanation

Objective 5.2.3

If you have a conflict—perhaps you forgot to update your calendar with a prior commitment—you can decline a meeting request. When you do so, the organizer receives a message saying that you have declined the meeting request. Declined meeting requests will not be added to your calendar.

Canceling meetings

You can cancel a meeting if you were the organizer of it. Select it on your calendar and click Cancel Meeting on the Ribbon.

If all of the invited attendees have declined, you will be prompted to delete the meeting without sending cancellation notices. Otherwise, Outlook will send a cancellation notice to all invitees. That way, no one shows up for a canceled meeting.

If a meeting is canceled that you were planning to attend, you will receive a cancellation message. When the message arrives, click Remove from Calendar in the Reading pane to remove the meeting from your calendar. You can also open the message and click Remove from Calendar on the Ribbon.

Do it!

Objective 5.2.3

Students could open the message instead.

A-5:   Declining a meeting request

Here's how	Here's why
1 Activate Mail	
2 Select the **YY: Product Planning** message	(If necessary.) The contents of the meeting request appear in the Reading pane.
In the Reading pane, click **Decline**	To decline the meeting request from your partner. You are prompted with three options.
Observe the three options on the menu	You can edit the response; this would give you an opportunity to tell the organizer why you're declining the invitation. You can simply send the response. Or you can decline the meeting without sending a response.
3 Choose **Send the response now**	You have declined the invitation. It is removed from your Inbox.
4 Observe your Inbox	☒ **02: Product Planning** 🏳 Student02 11:12 AM
	After a moment, the decline response from your partner will show up in your Inbox.
5 Select the **Declined XX: Product Planning** message	The message states that your partner has declined the meeting request.
6 Activate the Calendar	
7 View tomorrow's schedule	Because you're the meeting organizer, the meeting is still in your calendar. If you don't want to have the meeting, you'll have to delete it from your calendar.
8 Select the **XX: Product Planning** meeting	
9 Click **Cancel Meeting**	Cancel Meeting
	To cancel the meeting and delete it from your calendar.
Select **Delete without sending a cancellation**	All invitees have declined, so there's no sense in sending a cancellation notice.
Click **OK**	The meeting is removed from your calendar.

Setting up recurring meetings

Explanation

Meetings that occur regularly are known as *recurring meetings*. For example, a quarterly sales meeting is a recurring meeting. You can schedule recurring meetings by setting recurrence options while adding the meeting to the Calendar.

Objective 5.2

Tell students that this is the same dialog box they would use to schedule recurring appointments or events.

Appointment Recurrence

Appointment time

Start: 12:00 PM

End: 12:30 PM

Duration: 30 minutes

Recurrence pattern

○ Daily   Recur every 1 week(s) on:

◉ Weekly   ☐ Sunday   ☐ Monday   ☑ Tuesday   ☐ Wednesday

○ Monthly   ☐ Thursday   ☐ Friday   ☐ Saturday

○ Yearly

Range of recurrence

Start: Tue 2/23/2010   ◉ No end date

   ○ End after: 10 occurrences

   ○ End by: Tue 4/27/2010

[OK] [Cancel] [Remove Recurrence]

Exhibit 7-3: The Appointment Recurrence dialog box

Required and optional attendees

For any type of meeting request, you can designate attendees as either required or optional. Required attendees must attend; if they cannot meet at the scheduled time, the meeting will have to be rescheduled. The meeting can proceed without optional attendees present.

When creating a meeting request, click the To button rather than typing addresses into the To box. Then select the required attendees and click Required. Select the optional attendees and click Optional. If you enter addresses into the To box, they are considered required attendees.

Do it!

A-6: Adding a recurring meeting

Objective 5.2

Here's how	Here's why
1 Switch to Month view	
2 Right-click the second Monday of the month	If that date is already past, select the second Monday of next month.
Choose **New Recurring Meeting**	To open the Appointment Recurrence dialog box. (You can also add a "normal" meeting and click Recurrence on the Ribbon.)

Partner B should select 10:00 AM.

3 Under Appointment time, from the Start list, select **9:00 AM**

From the Duration list, select **1 hour**

When you specify the duration, the end time is adjusted automatically.

4 Under Recurrence pattern, select **Monthly**

Set the recurrence pattern to the second Monday of every third month

| ⦿ The | second ▾ | Monday ▾ | of every | 3 | month(s) |

5 Click **OK**

To close the Appointment Recurrence dialog box.

Observe the Recurrence information beneath Location

(In the Untitled – Meeting window.) It displays the recurrence settings for the new meeting. You can change these settings by clicking the Recurrence button on the Ribbon.

6 Click **To**

To open the Select Attendees and Resources dialog box.

7 In the Name list, select your partner

Click **Required**

You'll make your partner a required attendee.

8 In the Name list, select **Instructor**

Click **Optional** and click **OK**

The Instructor will be invited as an optional attendee.

9 Specify the subject as **YY: Quarterly sales meeting**

Where *YY* is your lab station number.

Specify the location as **Conference Room**

In the Location box.

10 Send the meeting request

In Month view, there is no indicator that the meeting is a recurring meeting.

11 Click the second Monday's header

To switch to Day view for that day.

Observe the right edge of the meeting's box

| **01: Quarterly sales meeting** |
| Conference Room |
| student10   ↻ |

The circular double-arrow icon indicates a recurring meeting.

Proposing a new time for meetings

Explanation

Objective 5.2.4

If a meeting time does not fit your schedule, you can suggest an alternative time instead of declining the meeting. However, the meeting organizer will decide whether to reschedule the meeting or keep it at its originally proposed time. The organizer also controls whether or not attendees can propose a new time.

To propose a new time for the meeting:

1   Preview or open the meeting request message.

2   Click Propose New Time and select either Tentative and Propose New Time or Decline and Propose New Time to open the Propose New Time dialog box, shown in Exhibit 7-4. Here, you can modify the date and time, but you can't change the attendee list.

3   Modify the date and time, or choose AutoPick Next or click the << button to automatically select the next (or previous) available time for all attendees.

4   Click Propose Time to open a new Meeting Response window.

5   Click Send. The meeting organizer receives a New Time Proposed message.

You can propose a new time for a recurring meeting. You'll need to choose whether to propose a new time for a single occurrence or for the entire series when you open the request.

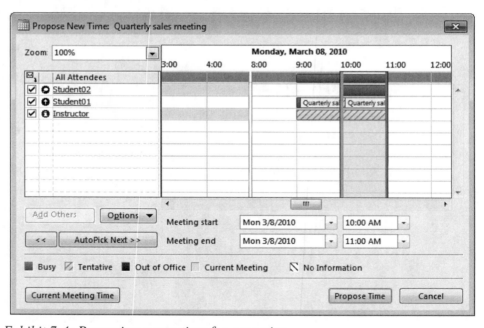

Exhibit 7-4: Proposing a new time for a meeting

A-7: Proposing a new time for a meeting

Here's how	Here's why
1 Double-click the **XX: Quarterly sales meeting** invitation	(Where *XX* is your partner's lab number.) Make sure you open the invitation your partner sent to you, not the one you sent to your partner.
Select **Open this occurrence** and click **OK**	You will propose a new time for just this one occurrence in the series.
Observe the buttons on the Ribbon	 As with the preview, you can use these buttons to respond to the request.
2 With your partner, decide which of you will propose one hour early and which of you will propose one hour later	You and your partner each invited the other to a recurring meeting. You'll reschedule both as you work together in this activity.
3 Click where indicated	 To display the menu.
Select **Tentative and Propose New Time**	To tentatively accept the meeting request but also propose a new time for the meeting. You can also use this menu to decline and propose a new time. (Clicking the top half of the button is the same as opening the menu and choosing Tentative and Propose New Time.)
Observe the time planner	It displays the calendar of all involved invitees and organizers.
4 If you're the partner proposing a later time, click **AutoPick Next**	To select the next available time slot for all attendees and resources.
If you're the partner proposing an earlier time, click **<<**	To the left of the AutoPick Next button.
5 Click **Propose Time**	To open a new Meeting Response window. It displays the meeting's original time and the new time proposed. You could enter a message to the organizer in the message body.
Click **Send**	To send your proposed new meeting time to your partner.

6 Open the **New Time Proposed:** *YY:* **Quarterly Sales Meeting** message	(Don't preview it.) The message states that your partner proposed a new time.
Click **Accept Proposal**	To accept the meeting time suggested by your partner and reschedule the meeting. The Meeting window appears.
Click **Send Update**	To send an update message to the attendees and close the Meeting window.
7 In your Inbox, select the *XX:* **Quarterly Sales Meeting** message	To preview it. You could also open the message.
8 Click **Accept**, and select **Send the Response Now**	On the Ribbon.
9 Activate the Calendar	
Switch to Month view	The meeting has been moved to the newly proposed time.
View the schedule for three months from now	The meeting invitation, which you've not accepted, is listed on the second Monday at its originally scheduled time. You rescheduled only the single occurrence in the series.

Remind students that the meeting their partner scheduled is also listed.

Modifying meetings

Explanation

Objective 5.2.2

You can modify meetings after scheduling them. When you do so, you will be prompted to resend the meeting request. If attendees accept the changes, the meeting will be rescheduled on everyone's calendar. You can modify both one-time and recurring meetings.

When you modify a recurring meeting, you can modify the entire series or a single occurrence of the meeting. Open the meeting and then select either "Open this occurrence" or "Open the series." Make your changes and click Send Update to send an update to the meeting attendees.

Do it!

Objective 5.2.2

A-8: Modifying a meeting

Here's how	Here's why
1 Confirm that you're viewing the calendar three months from now	
2 Double-click **YY: Quarterly sales meeting**	(Where *YY* is your lab number.) You'll modify this meeting. Because it's a recurring meeting, you'll be prompted to choose whether to change just this occurrence or the entire series.
Select **Open the series**	You want to change all occurrences of the meeting.
Click **OK**	
3 Click **Recurrence**	On the Ribbon.
4 If you're partner A, change the start time to **2:00 PM**	The End time is changed for you automatically because Outlook preserves the duration originally set for the meeting.
If you're partner B, change the start time to **3:00 PM**	
5 Click **OK**	A dialog box warns you that any exceptions associated with the recurring appointment will be canceled.
Click **OK**	To set all instances of the recurring appointment, including this month's, to the new time.
6 Click **Send Update**	To send an update to the attendees.

Partner B should schedule for 3:00 PM.

Topic B: Managing meetings

This topic covers the following Microsoft Office Specialist exam objectives for Outlook 2010.

#	Objective
5.2	**Create and manipulate meeting requests**
	5.2.2 Update a meeting request
	5.2.3 Cancel a meeting or invitation

Explanation

When creating meeting requests, you can reserve resources such as meeting rooms, overhead projectors, computers, and so forth. Reserving resources via meeting requests requires an Exchange Server or third-party components. Additionally, the Exchange administrator must create mailboxes for each resource or perform other configuration steps to enable resource scheduling.

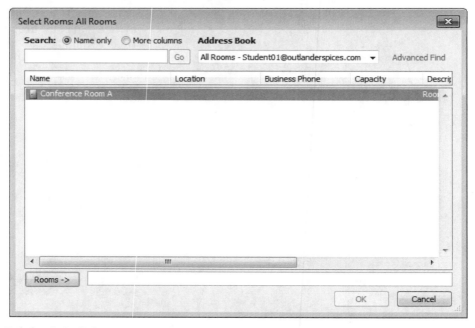

Exhibit 7-5: Selecting a room works like selecting invitees

To schedule a resource, you add it to the attendees list, just like you invite a person. If you're using the Scheduling Assistant, you can add the resource's calendar to your view to book a free time. If you frequently reserve a resource or you manage a resource, you might want to add its calendar to your Calendar folder.

B-1: Reserving resources in a meeting request

Here's how	Here's why
1 With your partner, decide who will be partner A and who will be partner B	Partner A will schedule appointments, events, and meetings at the times printed in the book. Partner B will schedule items at one hour *after* the times printed in the book.
2 Activate the Calendar	
3 Click **New Meeting**	To open a new Meeting window. The InfoBar tells you that invitations have not been sent for the meeting.
4 In the To box, enter your partner's e-mail address	
In the Subject box, enter **XX: Spice Sampling**	Where *XX* is your partner's number.
5 Next to the Location box, click **Rooms**	
6 Select **Conference Room A**	If necessary.
Click **Rooms** and click **OK**	

To...	Sally Sample; Conference Room A

The conference room is added to the To box.

Make sure partner B starts the meeting at 2:00.

7 Schedule the meeting to happen on next **Friday** at **1:00 PM**	Partner B, your meeting should start at 2:00 PM.
The meeting will last one hour	
8 Click **Send**	To send the meeting request and close the Meeting window.

Managing responses

Explanation

You need to know how the attendees of a meeting have responded so that you can decide whether to reschedule the meeting or change its venue. For example, if most of the attendees are not available at the proposed time, you'll need to reschedule the meeting or cancel it.

To review the responses of the attendees, open the Meeting window and click the Tracking button, shown in Exhibit 7-6. You can also check the InfoBar to see a summary of the responses, such as Accepted, Declined, or Tentative.

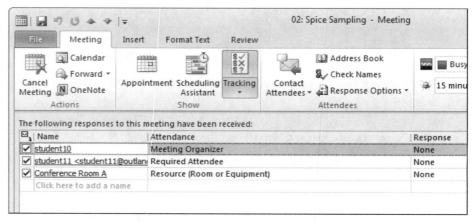

Exhibit 7-6: Meeting responses in the Tracking window

Do it!

B-2: Reviewing meeting responses

Here's how	Here's why
1 Open the **XX: Spice Sampling** meeting	(Double-click it.) Be sure to select the meeting for which you're the organizer. The InfoBar displays the number of attendees who have accepted, tentatively accepted, and declined your meeting request.
2 Click the top half of the Tracking button	Tracking To display a list of the invitees and their responses.
3 Close the window	

Adding and removing attendees

Explanation

Objective 5.2.2

You can add and remove meeting attendees as needed. To do so:

1 Open the meeting.

2 To add or remove attendees, either edit the entries in the To box, or click the To button and use the resulting window.

3 Click Send Update, and choose whether to send the update to just the attendees who were added or removed or to all attendees.

4 Click OK.

Do it!

Objective 5.2.2

B-3:   Adding meeting attendees

Here's how	Here's why
1 Open the *XX*: **Spice Sampling** meeting	Be sure to select the meeting for which you're the organizer. The InfoBar displays the number of attendees who have accepted, tentatively accepted, and declined your meeting request.
2 Click **To**	
Select **Instructor**	
Click **Required**	
Click **OK**	
3 Click **Send Update**	
4 Select **Send updates only to added or deleted attendees**	(If necessary.) You can also opt to send the update to all attendees.
Click **OK**	Only the new attendee will receive the meeting update.

Communicating with attendees

Explanation

Sometimes you need to send additional information to attendees. Perhaps you received a new report that attendees should review before the meeting. You can send a note to attendees by opening the meeting item, clicking Contact Attendees, and choosing New E-mail to Attendees. Compose your message as usual and click Send.

Do it!

B-4: Contacting meeting attendees

Here's how	Here's why
1 Open the **XX: Spice Sampling** meeting	Be sure to select the meeting for which you're the organizer. The InfoBar displays the number of attendees who have accepted, tentatively accepted, and declined your meeting request.
2 Click **Contact Attendees**	![Contact Attendees button]
Choose **New E-mail to Attendees**	
3 In the message area, enter **Please bring bottled water or another drink. We'll have many spices to sample.**	
4 Click **Send**	
5 Close the Meeting window	

Canceling meetings

Explanation

Objective 5.2.3

To cancel a meeting, open it or preview it. Click Cancel Meeting on the Ribbon. Then click Send Cancellation to send the cancellation notice to all attendees.

If a meeting is canceled that you were planning to attend, you will receive a cancellation message. When the message arrives, click Remove from Calendar in the Reading pane to remove the meeting from your Calendar. You can also open the message and click Remove from Calendar on the Ribbon.

You cannot cancel a meeting without sending a cancellation message. This requirement prevents attendees from showing up for a canceled meeting.

Do it!

Objective 5.2.3

B-5: Canceling a meeting

Here's how	Here's why
1 Activate Mail	If necessary.
2 Select the **YY: Spice Sampling** meeting request	You will accept your partner's meeting request so that you can both observe the e-mail messages exchanged when a meeting is canceled.
Click **Accept** and choose **Send the Response Now**	To accept the invitation.
3 Activate the Calendar	
4 Open the **XX: Spice Sampling** meeting	
5 Click **Cancel Meeting**	
Click **Send Cancellation**	
6 Activate Mail	If necessary.
7 Open or preview the **Canceled: XX: Spice Sampling** message	The meeting has been canceled.
Click **Remove from Calendar**	To delete the meeting from your Calendar.
8 Activate the Calendar	
Observe next Friday's schedule	The canceled meeting has been removed.

Unit summary: Meeting requests and responses

Topic A   In this topic, you used the Calendar to **plan a meeting**. You created and sent a **meeting request**, which contains all of the details of a meeting proposal, such as time, date, and subject. You learned how to accept or decline a meeting request. You also proposed a new time for the meeting.

Topic B   In this topic, you learned how to **reserve resources** and **review responses**. You also learned how to update a meeting, add and remove meeting attendees, and send additional information to attendees. Next, you learned how to **cancel** a meeting.

Independent practice activity

In this activity, you'll create and send a meeting request. You'll also open a meeting request, propose a new time, and accept a proposed time change.

1 Create a meeting request with the subject *XX*: **Worldwide sales strategy** for next Tuesday at an hour of your choosing. Send the meeting request to your partner.

2 Open the meeting request that you receive from your partner.

3 Propose a new time, and send the meeting request.

4 Accept the proposal.

5 Close Outlook.

Review questions

1 What is a meeting request?

A meeting request is a special type of message that contains details of a proposed meeting time.

2 What are the four types of meeting attendees?

Meeting organizer, required attendee, optional attendee, and resource

3 How do you accept a meeting request?

Open or preview the meeting request message and click Accept.

4 True or false? When you decline a meeting request, an entry is added to your calendar so that you can join the meeting later if you change your mind.

False. If you decline a meeting, it is not added to your calendar. You can tentatively accept a meeting if you think you might attend and you want an entry added to your calendar.

5 Do you always have the option of proposing a new date and time if you are invited to a meeting that doesn't work with your schedule?

The meeting organizer controls whether attendees can propose a new meeting date or time. You can propose a new time whenever the Propose New Time button is available.

6 How do you add or remove a meeting attendee?

Open the meeting window. Edit the To box, or click To and add or remove attendees. Click Send Update and specify whether you want to send the update to the added or removed attendees or to all attendees.

7 As the meeting organizer, how can you easily see all of the invitees' responses to your meeting request?

Open the meeting and click the Tracking button on the Ribbon.

8 When you cancel a meeting that you created, can you choose whether Outlook should deliver cancellation notices to the other attendees?

No. Outlook sends cancellation notices automatically.

9 True or false? Your Exchange administrator must configure resources, such as rooms and equipment, before you can reserve them via meeting requests.

True.

10 What is the benefit of using the Scheduling Assistant when creating a meeting request?

You can view the calendars of all of the attendees so that you can select a time when everybody is free.

11 To use Schedule view to see other people's calendars, you must first do what?

Add their calendars to your Calendar folder.

Course summary

This summary contains information to help you bring the course to a successful conclusion. Using this information, you will be able to:

A Use the summary text to reinforce what students have learned in class.

B Direct students to the next courses in this series (if any), and to any other resources that might help students continue to learn about Microsoft Outlook 2010.

Topic A: Course summary

At the end of the class, use the following summary text to reinforce what students have learned. It is intended not as a script, but rather as a starting point.

Unit summaries

Unit 1

In this unit, students learned about the common elements of the **Outlook 2010 user interface**, such as the Ribbon, Navigation pane, Reading pane, and To-Do Bar. Students customized Outlook Today. And finally, they used Outlook's **Help** system.

Unit 2

In this unit, students learned how to compose and send **e-mail messages**. Then students previewed and **opened** the messages to read them. Students also forwarded, **replied** to, and deleted messages. Students then learned how to include **attachments** with their messages.

Unit 3

In this unit, students set importance and sensitivity levels for messages and requested delivery and read **receipts**. Students also learned how to manage **junk e-mail**. Next, they learned how to use **Search folders**. Finally, students learned how to **print** messages.

Unit 4

In this unit, students learned how to manage **contacts** and the Contacts folder. They added, edited, and organized contacts. Students also created a **contact group**. Finally, they explored the **People Pane** to view contact details.

Unit 5

In this unit, students learned how to manage **tasks** and the Tasks folder. They created **one-time** and **recurring** tasks. Students also learned how to **assign** tasks and how to accept and decline task requests. Finally, students sent status updates and **tracked** the completion of a task.

Unit 6

In this unit, students learned how to use the **Calendar** to set up one-time and recurring **appointments**. Students also learned how to modify, delete, and restore appointments. Students then learned how to add one-time and recurring **events**. Finally, students customized the Calendar views and added **holidays** to the Calendar.

Unit 7

In this unit, students learned how to use the Calendar to send **meeting requests**. They scheduled one-time and recurring meetings. Students also learned how to accept and decline meeting requests, as well as **propose new times** for meetings. Students then learned how to **reserve resources**, such as meeting rooms. Finally, students learned how to **update** and **cancel** meetings.

Topic B: Continued learning after class

Point out to your students that it is impossible to learn how to use any software effectively in a single day. To get the most out of this class, students should begin using Microsoft Outlook to perform real tasks as soon as possible. We also offer resources for continued learning.

Next courses in this series

This is first course in this series. The next courses in this series are:

- *Outlook 2010: Intermediate*
  - Customize Outlook and create and use Quick Steps and shortcuts
  - Apply themes and stationary and use message options, such as voting buttons
  - Search and filter messages, and use categories
  - Create and use public folders
  - Create and use views, and create rules to manage messages automatically
- *Outlook 2010: Advanced*
  - Use the Outlook Social Connector and RSS feeds
  - Manage your mailbox and archive messages
  - Create and work with notes and Journal entries
  - Share calendars and contacts
  - Use Mail Merge and e-mail templates

Other resources

For more information, visit www.axzopress.com.

Glossary

Address book
A database that contains the names and contact information for people with whom you frequently communicate.

Appointment
A time slot that you reserve on your calendar, such as for a dentist appointment.

Attachment
A file that is transmitted along with an e-mail message so the recipient can see the file in its original format.

Contact
A person with whom you have a business or a personal relationship. You can manage information about each contact, such as the person's name, address, telephone number, e-mail address, Web site address, company name, birthday, and anniversary.

Contact group
A group of e-mail addresses under a single entry, enabling you to send one message to multiple recipients. (Called a "distribution list" in previous versions of Outlook.)

Contacts folder
Also referred to as the *Outlook Address Book*, an address book that is private for each user. You can use your Contacts folder to add e-mail addresses and other information for the people with whom you frequently communicate.

Date Navigator
A miniature calendar that's used to select a date to be displayed in the Calendar. The To-Do bar also contains a Date Navigator.

E-mail
An electronic message sent from one computer to another.

E-mail account
A record that contains the information that identifies a user so that he or she can send and receive e-mail messages. A user can have more than one e-mail account. To access an e-mail account, a user needs a user name and a password.

E-mail postmarking
A feature that incorporates a digital postmark into messages to help reduce the amount of spam in your Inbox. Messages without postmarks are sent to the Junk E-Mail folder.

Event
An activity that lasts for a period of one or more days and that can be added to the Calendar.

Folder pane
The middle pane of the Outlook window; it displays the Folder Contents list.

Global Address List
An Exchange Server address book that contains all of the users, groups, and contact-group e-mail addresses in your organization. All users in an organization have access to the Global Address List. Only the Exchange Server administrators can edit this address book.

Importance
The priority of a message. When you set the Importance level of a message to High, the red exclamation mark that's added tells the recipient that the message needs an immediate response.

Inbox
A folder that contains all of the messages you receive. You can read, create, reply to, forward, and delete messages in this folder.

InfoBar
An area, located at the top of a message in the Reading pane or Message window, that indicates the action taken on the message, along with the date and time.

Item
Any e-mail message, contact, or task created in Outlook. Items are stored in folders, such as Inbox, Calendar, Contacts, Tasks, and Notes.

Junk e-mail
Unsolicited messages, such as business promotions, advertisements, and messages with adult content. Also called "spam."

Meeting request
An invitation that contains the details of a meeting proposal, such as time, date, and subject. These invitations are sent by e-mail to the invitees.

Message flag
A flag symbol, located to the right of a message in the Folder Contents list, that identifies the message for further action. When you flag a message, you can specify the action to be taken, the due date, and the time.

Navigation pane

The leftmost pane in the Outlook window. It shows the active pane and contains pane-switching buttons.

Outlook Address Book

An address book that contains a private list of e-mail addresses and is automatically created from the contacts in your Contacts folder. When you update the contact information, the Outlook Address Book is updated automatically.

Range of recurrence

The period defined by the starting and ending dates of a recurring task or appointment.

Reading pane

A pane in the Outlook window that displays e-mail messages.

Recurrence pattern

The frequency with which a task or appointment occurs. For example, the task or appointment can occur annually, monthly, weekly, or daily.

Recurring appointment

An appointment or meeting that occurs regularly.

Recurring task

A task that needs to be performed on a regular basis.

Search folders

Folders used to locate messages in a specific category or based on a specific condition.

Sensitivity

A message classification that indicates messages containing personal or highly sensitive content. There are four levels of sensitivity: Confidential, Private, Personal, and Normal (default).

SharePoint Services

A technology that enables aggregation, collaboration, and search capabilities for people, teams, and information.

Task

An Outlook item that keeps track of activities that must be completed within a specified period of time. A task has a current status, which can be In Progress, Not Started, Waiting on someone else, Deferred, or Completed.

Task list

A section of the To-Do Bar that displays the tasks for the current date.

Task request

An e-mail message asking the recipient to complete a task.

Tasks folder

The folder that's used to create tasks and monitor their status.

To-Do Bar

A pane in the Outlook window that displays the Date Navigator, upcoming appointments, and tasks.

View

The way data appears in a folder. Examples include Day view and Month view in the Calendar.

Index

A

Address books, 2-10
Appointments
    Creating, 6-4
    Creating from e-mail messages, 6-10
    Deleting and restoring, 6-15
    Marking as private, 6-5
    Recurring, 6-8, 6-14
    Rescheduling, 6-12
Attachments, 2-30
    Reading, 2-36
    Saving, 2-36

B

Bcc box, 2-7
Blocked Senders list, 3-16

C

Calendar
    Adding holidays to, 6-29
    Adding time zones to, 6-28
    Printing, 6-31
    Setting defaults for, 6-26
    Shortcuts for using, 6-24
    Switching views of, 6-20
Calendar folder, adding other calendars to, 7-8
Calendar pane, 1-9, 6-2
Contact groups
    Creating, 4-17
    Modifying, 4-20
    Using, 4-18
Contacts
    Adding, 4-4
    Adding from same company, 4-9
    Attaching items to, 4-8
    Editing, 4-7
    Printing, 4-16
    Sending, 4-11
Contacts folder, 1-13, 4-2
    Views of, 4-13
Contacts pane, 1-9
Control menu, 2-5

D

Daily Task list, 6-2
Delayed e-mail delivery, 3-6
Deleted Items folder, 1-13, 2-27
Delivery receipts, 3-9

Dialog Box Launcher, 3-2
Distribution lists, 4-17
Drafts folder, 1-13

E

Electronic business cards, changing, 4-14
E-mail address, specifying for replies, 3-8
Events
    Adding, 6-16
    Marking as private, 6-16
    Recurring, 6-18

F

Flagging messages, 3-11
Folder Contents list, icons in, 2-2
Folder List pane, 1-9
Folder pane, 1-4
Folders, default, 1-12

H

Help system, 1-25
HMTL message format, 2-7
Holidays, adding to Calendar, 6-29
Hyperlinks, inserting, 2-25

I

Images, inserting or attaching, 2-33
Inbox folder, 1-13, 2-2

J

Journal folder, 1-13
Journal pane, 1-9
Junk E-mail filter, 3-16
Junk E-mail folder, 1-13, 3-15
Junk-email, options for managing, 3-17

M

Mail pane, 1-9
Meeting requests
    Creating, 7-2
    Declining, 7-12
    Reading, 7-6
Meeting responses, viewing, 7-22
Meeting window, opening, 7-2
Meetings
    Adding and removing attendees, 7-23
    Canceling, 7-12, 7-25

Proposing new time for, 7-16
Recurring, 7-14
Required vs. optional attendees, 7-14
Rescheduling, 7-19
Reserving resources for, 7-20
Scheduling, 7-10
Message headers, 2-2
Messages
Attaching files to, 2-30
Checking spelling and grammar in, 2-14
Creating, 2-6
Deleting and restoring, 2-27
Flagging, 3-11
Forwarding, 2-23
Importance levels of, 3-3
Including images in, 2-33
Marking as completed, 3-12
Plain text vs. HTML, 2-7
Printing, 3-22
Read receipts for, 3-9
Replying to, 2-20
Sending, 2-8
Sending blind copies of, 2-7
Sensitivity levels for, 3-2
Mini toolbar, 2-12
Multi-day events, 6-16

N

Names, checking, 2-10
Navigation pane, 1-4, 1-8
Collapsing and expanding, 1-10
Notes folder, 1-13
Notes pane, 1-9

O

Outbox folder, 1-13
Outlook
Help system, 1-25
Integration with Word, 2-10
Window components, 1-2
Outlook Options dialog box, 5-20, 6-26
Outlook Social Connector, 4-23
Outlook Today page, 1-13, 1-20
Customizing, 1-22

P

Page setup, changing, 3-23
Panes
Default, 1-8
Expanding and collapsing, 1-5
Resizing, 1-5
Switching among, 1-4
Paste options, 2-16
People Pane, 4-23, 4-25, 4-27
Print options, 3-22

Q

Quick Access toolbar, 1-3, 2-5

R

Read receipts, 3-9
Reading pane, 1-4, 1-16
Recurring appointments, 6-8, 6-14
Recurring events, 6-18
Recurring meetings, 7-14
Recurring tasks, 5-8
Reminders window, 3-14
Ribbon, 1-3
Context-sensitive, 1-15
RSS feeds, 1-13

S

Safe Senders list, 3-16
Schedule view, 6-22, 7-8
Scheduling Assistant, 7-10
Search folders, 1-13
Adding, 3-19
Using, 3-21
Sensitivity, setting for e-mail, 3-2
Sent Items folder, 1-13
Shortcuts pane, 1-9
Social networks, connecting to, 4-23
Spelling, checking, 2-14
Status reports, sending, 5-17

T

Task requests, 5-12
Accepting or declining, 5-14
Tasks
Assigning, 5-12, 5-14
Changing settings for, 5-20
Creating, 5-4
Deleting, 5-5
Editing, 5-7
Marking as completed, 5-10
Printing, 5-21
Recurring, 5-8
Sending status reports on, 5-17
Tracking, 5-19
Views of, 5-11
Tasks folder, 5-2
Tasks pane, 1-9, 5-2
Time zones, adding to calendar, 6-28
To-Do Bar, 1-4, 1-18, 5-2

V

Views
For tasks, 5-11
In Calendar, 6-20